PETER JACKSON'S
KING KONG
THE OFFICIAL GAME OF THE MOVIE

D1223838

TABLE OF CONTENTS

INTRODUCING:

THE 8TH WONDER OF THE WORLD

Prepare yourself for delights, wonders, fear, and amazement as the cast and crew aboard the Venture ship discover Skull Island, a place know to exist only in myth. What you see along this journey is second to nothing, and the only certainty is that there are surprises around every turn. Dangerous creatures, savage natives, the 8th wonder of the world, and the environment of Skull Island are only unified in their ability to protect this majestic place from outsides, but fate has given us this opportunity.

There are 40 areas of traps, creatures, and carnage on the way through Skull Island and beyond, and this guide gives players the chance to make the most of them! Compiled here are tips for higher-tier gameplay, all of the strategies for completing the levels, notes for improving one's score after the game is completed, the ways to unlock extra content, and all of the tricks it takes to become a better player in subsequent runs through the island.

Read on, if you dare to face Skull Island and all its peril.

HOW TO USE THIS GUIDE

This chapter briefly explains what readers should expect from the various sections of the guide. Start here to learn where to look for the walkthrough, game strategies, and so forth.

THE SCRIPT

The Script is a chapter about the game's story. Don't worry; nothing about either the game or the movie is going to be spoiled.

CASTING CALL

All of the game's characters are shown and explained here. Each person has their own motivations, style of action, and ability to contribute to the team, so it's worth knowing who they are.

STAGE DIRECTIONS

In this chapter, the guide turns toward more tactical matters. The control systems for the game and how they are best used are examined in detail. This chapter is NOT a rehash of button controls or key mappings; it is a platform-independent analysis of what the controls accomplish

PROPS

Characters in the game use a number of weapons and tools to make it through Skull Island intact. This chapter lists those items, how to use them, and goes into some of the strategies behind the equipment. Players hoping to make a more careful run through the game (especially during a second playthrough) are likely to gain a great deal from this section.

THE ANTAGONISTS

Each of the enemies on Skull Island has a style of attacking that is much easier to counter once a player understands what is happening. This chapter is a bestiary that lists the strengths, weaknesses, and oddities of each creature on the island.

MASTERING YOUR PART

More involved aspects of gameplay and strategy are covered in this chapter; learning how to use characters to their fullest, getting through levels without a scratch, how to access bonus features, and other treats and written here.

AN EPIC ENDEAVOR

Of course, the walkthrough for the game is the feature presentation. Find out where to run, what to burn, and which enemies to shoot.

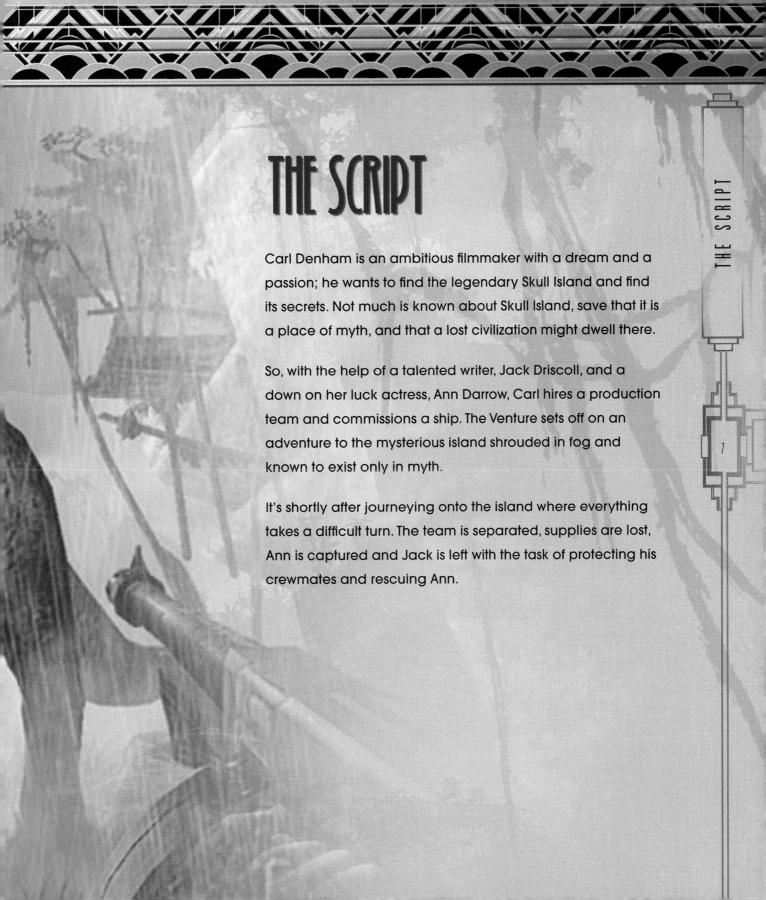

THE SCRIPT

Carl Denham is an ambitious filmmaker with a dream and a passion; he wants to find the legendary Skull Island and find its secrets. Not much is known about Skull Island, save that it is a place of myth, and that a lost civilization might dwell there.

So, with the help of a talented writer, Jack Driscoll, and a down on her luck actress, Ann Darrow, Carl hires a production team and commissions a ship. The Venture sets off on an adventure to the mysterious island shrouded in fog and known to exist only in myth.

It's shortly after journeying onto the island where everything takes a difficult turn. The team is separated, supplies are lost, Ann is captured and Jack is left with the task of protecting his crewmates and rescuing Ann.

CASTING CALL

When trying to survive the attacks of dinosaurs, gigantic beasts, natives, and nature itself, Jack Driscoll is going to need all the help he can get. This chapter shows the characters in the game and what they can do to help get through Skull Island.

JACK DRISCOLL

Jack Driscoll is a writer who has luckily stayed in fairly good shape and knows how to throw pointy objects! He is coming to Skull Island with Carl to write the script for the next Carl Denham Picture. This is the protagonist for the game, and he is capable of great feats. Jack can throw, shoot various weapons, burn through barricades, and hide from wild beasts. It's all in a day's work.

CARL DENHAM

Carl Denham is a filmmaker without the same gift of common sense that most of the team members possess. He is drawn to Skull Island by glory and mystique, and the physical dangers of the region seem trivial to him. Safely behind the lens of a camera,

Carl films and shouts orders, so he won't be as much help in a fight as some of the other team members.

ANN DARROW

Ann Darrow was chosen to come with the team at the last minute. She is a vaudville actress eager to make a picture that Jack Driscoll is writing, She has stamina, and knows how to take care of herself even when things go wrong. Gifted with compassion

and courage, she is dependable under any circumstance.

Because of these things, Ann is very useful to have nearby in various levels. She is more aggressive with throwing Spears and Bones, and her ability to climb to more distant locations makes her indispensable. Ann's only downside is that she is so pretty that every person and creature on Skull Island wants to grab her for one reason or another. Ann is a bright woman, but it is STILL a tough job keeping her safe.

HAYES

Hayes was a great person to select for this trip, because he is strong and level-headed. From the very beginning, Hayes takes a sensible attitude about what needs to be done, who needs to do it, and how to improve everyone's chances for making it

home. His presence is further enhanced by his training in various weapons; Hayes grabs Spears, Bones, Rifles, Pistols, etc. If something can be thrown or fired at any enemy, Hayes is ready to take it and make use of it.

When Hayes is around, he acts in support of Jack's actions, and he is also a second set of hands for carrying higher-powered weaponry. If Jack runs out of ammo with his weapon, Hayes is tough enough to trade down and toss Jack whatever he is carrying. This makes it possible to have more weapons available than Jack could carry on his own.

CAPTAIN ENGLEHORN

Captain Englehorn is the captain of the Venture ship who has heard of the dangers and mysteries of Skull Ilsland. He is experience with seaplanes turns out to be even more important than everyone imagined! Because the water landing on Skull Island has a few problems, the way back to the ship might be dependent on Captain Englehorn's ability to land in any large body of water, inland or out at sea.

Also, Englehorn is the only person with the ability to get supplies in to the team. Even when he cannot land, the captain is willing to make dangerously low passes over the jungle with crates of weapons and ammo. He drops these with fine precision! Jack and the others are always on the lookout for these care packages, and the buzzing of Captain Englehorn's propellers is most auspicious.

PRESTON

Preston was on a different boat heading toward the island, so his team is separated from Jack, Ann, Carl, and Hayes. The second group, with Preston, Lumpy, and Jimmy is off on their own, status unknown.

LUMPY THE COOK

Back when the team was being assembled, it seemed quite important to have a good cook along (to keep everyone's morale high and their bellies full). After the disastrous landing, it's hard to say whether any of that will be important.

JIMMY

Jimmy is a young man and a scrapper! Though daunted by being surrounded with experienced folks, he does his best to do what is right and keep himself focused. Jimmy doesn't have any weapon experience at his age, but like many of the others he is able to pick up a Spear or Bone in hope of a lucky toss.

KING KONG

King Kong is one of the greatest mysteries of Skull Island, he appears to be about 100 years old, the last of his kind, and is about 25 feet tall. Kong is a creature to be respected and feard. He can charge over great distance, leap from cliff to cliff with ease, swipe aside man and beast alike without pause and is the only creature on the island that measures up against the V-Rex in battle.

STAGE DIRECTIONS

It takes little more than a minute or two to learn this game's control system; both Jack and Kong are easy to use and mastery is only a few hours away with some solid practice. However, this chapter explains many of the overt tricks and subtleties that help to use the controls to their fullest! Why not hit the ground running on Skull Island?

STANDARD CONTROLS

CONTROLLING JACK

The majority of levels are spent as Jack, in first-person mode. Movement and most of the action is similar in feel to a number of modern shooters, and high accuracy is of the utmost importance. Whether playing on a console or PC, it is very useful to have the best control system possible (good controller, high-end mouse, and so forth). This is true for all action games; refined controls for shooting make accuracy so much better that it's a world of change.

MOVEMENT

Movement is extremely simple for Jack; walk forward or backward, strafe left or right. Jack throws, looks, and shoots in the same direction, so things are streamlined whether you are using a mouse and keyboard or a controller. Most of the time, it's best to have Jack run at full speed; there is no endurance bar or other limitation to Jack's movement (though he'll need to breathe heavily after a time, which is distinctly audible).

Dodging is best done with strafing and moving backwards at the same time against most enemies. This gives Jack more time to take down enemies such as creatures. Megapedes are better to just strafe against, as they are good at covering distance but cannot retarget mid-flight. Running monsters, such as V-Rexes and Venatosauruses, are better to distract or turn away from (to run at Jack's full speed toward shelter).

AIMING

As stated, Jack throws/shoots where he is looking. Whether the aiming visor is up or down, the weapons are going to hit targets that are roughly down the center of the screen. Only with hurled weapons (the Bone and Spear) is it necessary to account for a substantial effect from gravity; none of the projectile weapons are firing over enough range to be affected in that way.

If aiming is a problem, check the sensitivity of the device you are using (note that this isn't always an option, as it depends on the platform). Dodging and turning are greatly improved by setting devices to higher sensitivity. Aiming and accuracy are improved by lowering the sensitivity until it reaches a certain point; this point is best found through testing, and varies from weapon to weapon. Look for a sensitivity that allows enough defense to keep Jack out of trouble while giving adequate responsiveness with a variety of weaponry.

CROUCH

Crouching rarely comes into play on Skull Island, but Jack gains benefits from this in a few, specific places. When the team is trying to be stealthy and avoid the detection of Venatosauruses, crouching has its benefits. This action slows Jack down, which is why it isn't normally used; in many cases, fast travel is the key to survival.

READY WEAPON/FIRE WEAPON

Firing weapons and throwing objects is a two-stage task. The first control readies the object (bringing the weapon to bear or pulling back Jack's arm for a throw). At that time, the firing control is used to shoot a single round or throw the weapon.

For greater accuracy, ready a weapon then use the zoom control. Zooming brings the target into greater focus and allows for use of various weapons at substantial range. In the specific case of the Sniper Rifle, zooming is used to access the scope feature of the item.

Trying to fire a weapon without readying it first causes Jack to jab or swing with the item he is carrying. This doesn't do noticeable damage to targets, but is instead used to ward off enemies. Push aside incoming attackers and break through obstacles using this control.

RELOAD

Firing a weapon after its clip is empty starts the reloading process, but this isn't always a wise time to reload; after all, if you were squeezing the trigger, it might mean that you wanted to shoot something. Something big. Something that is about to munch on your pancreas. That is NOT the best of times to be reloading a weapon.

Thus, it's sensible to reload weapons between battles, whether Jack's clip is empty or not. Pick a time that seems safe and reload, even if Jack is only short by a round or two.

CLIP QUERY

Without the inventory option chosen, you aren't going to know how many bullets/shells Jack is carrying. That can be very dangerous, and it is worrisome when deciding whether to take one weapon or another (after coming upon a crate). Use this command to figure out how many clips Jack is carrying. As long as he has enough to get back, there is nothing to worry about!

DROP WEAPON

If Jack has an object in his hands other than a projectile weapon (e.g. Bones and Spears), this command drops that item onto the ground and allows Jack to ready his primary weapon instead. This is useful when a sudden threat is too great to be handled with a Bone, or when Jack is carrying a lever back to a gate and is ambushed.

INTERACT WITH CHARACTERS

Jack can get weapons from other characters on the team. Interact with them and he'll ask the person to throw him the weapon that they are carrying. If Jack already has a weapon, he'll toss it to them in exchange. Interacting with Hayes is especially useful, as he often carries another projectile weapon instead of a Bone or Spear. Thus, he acts as a secondary inventory slot for Jack even when he isn't in battle. It's good to have buddies.

Controlling Kong

King Kong is meant to be fun to control in every way. Most of his levels are somewhat less difficult than Jack's areas, and the fighting is much more assertive. This draws less from survival shooters and more from general action games. The view shifts to a third-person perspective, and all the fury of Kong is at your disposal. Enjoy!

Swat

Kong's basic attack is a swat that knocks small enemies into oblivion and stops heavier targets in their tracks, stunning them briefly. This isn't a strong enough attack to outright kill the V-Rexes and other brutal predators of the island, but it is a good way of gaining initiative against them. For creatures and natives, however, a swat is more than enough to send them flying!

Note that Kong can still swat at things under challenging circumstances. When Kong has an arm tied up with climbing or carrying someone, he still has the wherewithal to slap at pests that try to bother him. If creatures or other nuisance monsters attack during such times, ward them off instead of letting them get a free lunch on Kong's back.

Charge/Jump

Kong races forward when the charge controls are used. If he comes to an area where a jump is possible, the same control forces him to leap. This makes it easy to race through levels by pushing in a single direction and tapping the charge control to get there, whether by land or air.

When charging, Kong gathers the momentum to unleash a mean charge attack! This strike deals more damage, stuns enemies for a longer period if they survive at all, and looks very cool. Charge attacks are a truly fast way to make it through barricades; Kong doesn't need to stop and swat at the structures. Indeed, he can run at them at full speed and break right through.

Kong can also attack while jumping. Because many of his enemies aren't as mobile, it's often an option for Kong to leap away from there in certain areas, then to return aggressively.

GRAB/THROW

Once Kong grabs an enemy, he has a chance for an outright kill (against almost anything). Light targets, such as creatures, are easy to grab. Use the command, watch Kong grab the enemy, then throw them at something that needs to take damage. Kong can grab creatures, cars, stones, trees, and just about anything that IS or ISN'T nailed down. Good for him. Bad for his enemies.

But this command is even more important than that. Larger foes, like V-Rexes are killed via a successful grapple. Weaken the creatures by charging and attacking them, especially when Kong is in a fury. When the enemies are weakened or knocked down, grapple them and tap the controls very quickly to have Kong destroy them. If an enemy ever grapples Kong, the controls also need to be tapped, though in this case to save Kong's life.

INCITE FURY

Kong has more impact and is harder to damage when he is furious. To drive Kong into this state for a short time, use this command he'll beat on his chest. Keep tapping the control until the screen changes appearance. Once that completes, tear into any and all threats until nothing remains of them but a bloody pulp.

If Kong is attacked while driving himself into a fury, the act is disrupted. Run away from enemies temporarily or start a fury while the foes are distracted, stunned, and such.

There are no downsides to Kong's fury. It wears off eventually but can be started again immediately. As long as Kong doesn't get extensive therapy, he has more than enough angst to go around.

OPTIONS

AUDIO

The audio options for the game are straight forward. Set the volume to the level that you feel is appropriate, and decide whether to keep subtitles off or on. The voice acting is extremely clear and consistent, even during intense scenes (if that makes a difference for you).

VIDEO

The visual formats for the game follow movie conventions. The 16/9 setting offers the standard setting for older monitors and televisions, but the game can be set to 4/3 (with or without black bands) for a more cinematic feel. This is available regardless of the display system you are using.

The special mode that can be unlocked is for an "Old Movie" filter. This causes the game to look like a black and white picture from the older days of film. This increases the difficulty slightly because the visual cues are somewhat off from what players are probably used to. That is actually a bit of a side benefit for secondary play!

Finally, the option to flip the horizontal axis is given after players defeat the game for the first time. All of the left/right aspects of the game are reverse, so people who have learned the levels by heart are going to have major problems while they get used to things. Again, this is an added feature for difficulty that may appeal to players on their second, third, and subsequent runs through the game.

Control options

There are standard features in here, such as vibration control (purely a personal preference), and the option to invert the aiming axis. Decide what you are interested in and run with it.

The more exciting aspects are the options to enable an aiming visor and Jack's inventory. By default, there is no interface at all on the game screen, adding to the feel that you ARE playing as Jack on the first person levels. These options change that.

The aiming visor lends a helping hand to players who are having targeting problems. A reticule appears onscreen when Jack raises a weapon, making it somewhat easier to hit foes at various ranges.

Putting the inventory onscreen makes it much easier to know exactly how many bullets/shells Jack is carrying at a given moment. Normally, the best you can do is to find out how many clips Jack has remaining, so this is a major improvement.

PROPS

Carl Denham's production team wasn't planning to take over Skull Island and declare the republic, so there are only a few weapons available to Jack and his allies. Most of the time, the scarce ammunition for these is like treasure to be hoarded and doled with care. Making the most of every bullet is of great importance for people with limited supplies in hostile territory. This chapter explains what the weapons are in this game and how to use them most effectively.

PISTOL

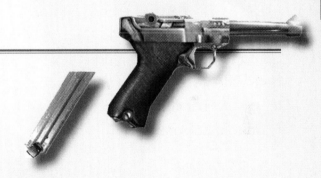

The Pistol has moderate stopping power, a fast firing rate, and sports a decent clip. That means it is often a good choice for unknown situations; the Pistol can handle close targets, somewhat distance targets, and both soft and heavy foes.

For all but the weakest enemies, two taps to the center of mass work perfectly. Megapedes, creatures, Venatosauruses, and other soft targets drop like lead from this, and it's a good middle ground between ammo conservation and risk of injury. Only of the only downsides to the Pistol is that more bullets are used per kill (compared to the Sniper Rifle). This only matters when trying for a high score on future playthroughs. In that case, every shot costs 100 points, and the Shotgun or Sniper Rifle are far better in that scenario.

The best situation of all for general fighting is to have Hayes carrying a Sniper Rifle or Shotgun, and Jack sporting the Pistol. That provides the flexibility to handle any situation well. If more firepower is needed, Jack and Hayes can trade weaponry. Otherwise, Jack can hurl Spears for immediate impact and use the Pistol as backup.

SHOTGUN

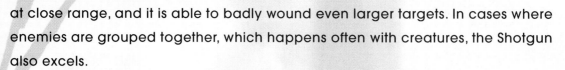

The Shotgun is extremely powerful at close range, and it is able to badly wound even larger targets. In cases where enemies are grouped together, which happens often with creatures, the Shotgun also excels.

Sadly, the Shotgun is only able to have several shells in its breach, and not many total shells can be carried at a time (nor are many found in each crate of supplies). So, the Shotgun is not a long-term solution that Jack can carry around. Instead, it's wise to take the Shotgun each time it is found, clear the area of any major problems, then return to the crate to swap back to whatever weapon Jack left there. This saves major ammunition with Jack's primary weapon and keeps the team safe.

The Shotgun is a very good weapon when trying for a high score; the impressive damage per shot ratio means that the Shotgun is able to clear enemies safely and without wasting many points. Though Spears are still the ultimate way to go for this style of fighting, a projectile weapon for fast and powerful aggression is an important backup.

Note that the Shotgun loses damage over range by a massive margin; this causes the weapon to be almost ineffective at anything beyond six or so paces. Sniping, covering allies, and other long-range tasks are VERY hard with the Shotgun, no matter how many shells Jack is carrying. Let the enemies close with the team to keep from wasting those precious shells.

SNIPER RIFLE

The Sniper Rifle is a connoisseurs' dream. Able to fire accurately over great distances, this weapon protects the team from Megapedes to other targets that are tricky to hit or prefer ambushes. One shot from the Sniper Rifle deals roughly twice the damage of a Pistol bullet, meaning that death is dealt faster and with fewer shots when the Sniper Rifle is used correctly.

The zoom feature on the Sniper Rifle automatically switches to a scope. This aids in hitting moving targets at long range. Taking down creatures that are hanging from cliffs or branches ahead is wise. This cuts down on the numbers for a pack and dramatically reduces the chance of Jack or a team member suffering an injury while fighting the enemies. When trying for a high score, preventing injury is essential! And, using a single bullet per kill isn't terribly inefficient even when it's compared to Spear throwing.

MACHINE GUN

Horribly inefficient for many fights, the Machine Gun is still the master of the field for throwing damage at a target. Each shot from it deals equivalent damage to a direct hit from a Pistol, and every clip for the weapon holds 30 bullets (it's just too bad that Captain Englehorn can't drop some of the larger drums for the Machine Gun)!

Foremost, squeeze the trigger on the Machine Gun and don't hold it down. Tap, tap. Tap, tap. Target dead, target dead. Don't get in to the fear or aggression and spray a target to death with 20 bullets. No matter what, it's very hard to hold on to Machine Gun ammo, and spraying means that the weapon is only likely to last a fight or two.

Much like the Shotgun, this weapon is a good choice for clearing an area then returning for Jack's original weapon. Because there aren't enough clips to go around, this isn't a long-term solution for the team's problems. Use the Machine Gun against rushes by Venatosauruses and other swarming foes.

BONE

Bones are found in piles across the entire island. These are never limited (Jack can keep drawing from the pile for days if he likes), and they don't deal terribly much damage per hit. Still, their accuracy is fair, especially when a practiced player zooms and gets a good feel for their target. Knocking urns of fire into thickets, nailing Megapedes, and other mundane chores are ideally suited for Bones.

These weapons can be set on fire to clear briars at range, set grass on fire (and harm the creatures lurking within), or to scare away creatures.

Master fast throwing with Bones for a surprising output of damage. The trick is to stand on a pile of Bones and fight from there. Done quickly, Jack can toss a Bone, grab another, and toss again with surprising speed and lethality. This technique can stop a rush by even larger predators (Jack can even say NO to a Venatosaurus with merely a pile of Bones).

SPEAR

Spears are handled in the same way as Bones, and they accomplish all of the same tasks. The perk is that Spears do more damage, being even more effective than Pistol shots for putting a stop to enemies. Spears are roughly equivalent to hits from a Sniper Rifle, making it possible to kill flying creatures and Megapedes with single shots. At worst, modest foes take two shots and spend so much time recovering from the first hit that a second blow is even easier to land.

Spears are found frequently in clusters; natives have placed them in bundles throughout the island. Look for those everyone and ALWAYS carry a Spear in hand when exploring. Being able to unleash practically free damage on any target that pops out is a gift from the heavens, and Jack won't waste any ammo doing it. Beyond that, Spears can be pulled out of targets and rethrown into the monsters for the kill. Venatosauruses, and groups of lesser beasts are all vulnerable to this.

When playing for a high score, Bones and Spears are better than projectile weapons. Each Bone or Spear thrown costs 20 points (compared to 100 points for a bullet/shell fired). Because the Spears have such high lethality, they are effectively five times more efficient than most equivalent weapons. It isn't worth taking an injury to use Spears instead of a projectile weapon because of the 1,000 point penalty per wound, but these thrown weapons ARE a critical way to improve already substantial scores. For more on this, Mastering Your Part has a section on improving scores and high-level playing.

LEVERS

Wooden stakes are used as levers throughout Skull Island. The villagers of the region have constructed heavy gates that aren't movable without using the pillars in front of them. Cleverly, these pillars are rotated by one or two people, allowing even the larger gates to be used in small groups.

Sometimes these levers aren't found at the gate itself. When that happens search the area for other pillars, off to the sides and such, and look for spare stakes. These are found without too much difficulty, as the natives NEVER take them too far away. They don't want their people to end up searching for a long time while V-Rexes are breaking through the ruins in search of grub.

THE ANTAGONISTS

Understanding the strengths and weaknesses of the enemies in this game is one of the best ways to improve a player's score in subsequent playthroughs! The first time through the game, it's possible to rely heavily on projectile weapons and use brute force to get through a number of the challenges. More refined play, however, is heavily dependent on a person's ability to predict enemy actions and use less firepower to greater effect. This chapter aids in that.

GIANT CRABS

The first enemies in the game are the Giant Crabs that live in and around the water. Also found in nearby caves, these beasts crawl slowly toward targets and try to lash out at them. Primarily, these are small targets that won't hassle anyone too much; they are easily dispatched with Bones or Spears at close or medium range, and anyone with room to back away from them needn't worry about being overwhelmed by numbers.

The larger form of the Giant Crabs take much more damage and have such potent shells that it's important to shoot to lower section of the creature. During the specific event in the game when Jack fights one of these, a Pistol is going to be handy, and that is the weapon of choice for the fight. There isn't as much room to maneuver, and using thrown Bones is very slow.

MEGAPEDES

Before long in the game, Megapedes are discovered. These creatures have the offensive advantage of being able to crawl over walls and ceilings, through tight places, and so forth. They can thus attack from almost any angle and retreat to safety while preparing another rush. Jack can defend himself from Megapedes can running to the side or directly away from the creatures when they gather to leap (this happens every time they attack). To

fully understand the attack sequence, watch a Megapede close in, listen for the telltale sound they make when gathering, and anticipate a jump within a second or so.

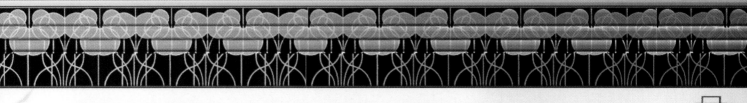

Spears work wonders on Megapedes. Wait for the creature to gather for its leap, thus immobilizing itself, then hurl the Spear into the body of the monster and watch it collapse. Quickly retrieve the weapon and use it to strike at the next millipede that comes along!

When points aren't an issue, the Sniper Rifle is a good weapon against the Megapedes; the high accuracy and damage of the weapon mean that single shots offer the kill. There are a few times when Jack is too far away from the actions to use Spears anyway, and he'll still need to defend allies from the Megapedes, so this is the weapon of choice.

FLYING CREATURES

Flying creatures are a constant source of danger and tension as the game progresses. These flying beasts are able to swoop in from high places and rake targets with their hind legs. Dodging these highly maneuverable foes is not the best idea; instead, a strong offense is the safest way to keep the team safe from creatures. There are two times when normal creatures are extremely exposed and are quickly dispatched: before leaving their flight patterns/ perches, and when slowing their approach.

Before creatures are aware of new food nearby, they either circle an area or find a place to perch upside down. Both of these situations are ideal because the creatures are so predictable. Use a Sniper Rifle, Pistol, or an Aimed Spear attack for a victory without any real effort! Also, stay calm if you see nearby creatures leaving their perches when an ally is shot at range; they DON'T often realize where the attack is coming from, and the creatures foolishly return to their perches before long.

31

The other weak time for a creature comes during their descent. Before raking their target, the creatures need to slow down and bring their legs forward. This presents a VERY large target for Jack to Spear, and it's hard to miss them. Don't dodge, don't run, and don't flinch. A single toss with a Spear is likely to do the trick, and it only takes a moment to pull the Spear out of the body for defending against another creature, so the technique works well even against groups.

The blue-hued big creatures are a more troublesome target. These older beasts have much hardier builds, are larger, and they are always accompanied by many of their children. Spears are useful for hassling big creatures at range, but their weakest time comes when they swoop down to claw at Jack. Unlike the smaller creatures, these big creatures tear directly through people, so it IS important to dodge. While doing so, fire the Shotgun or throw a Spear into the big creatures's face! One of the divine combinations is to have both the Spear and Shotgun ready, then to hit the big creaure at point blank with the Spear (stunning the beast). While it recovers, blast her two or three times with the Shotgun! The damage from this is extreme, and even these powerful predators can't survive much of that treatment.

SMALL CREATURES

Small creatures are a trivial threat. Surprisingly, they don't grow to immense size on Skull Island, and the variety found there aren't even terribly poisonous (they still are quite aggressive though). Often, creatures are found skittering around paths or items that Jack needs to use. Instead of fighting these groups, the key is to disperse the creatures and simply move on. Two actions accomplish this: using fire to ward off the creatures, and throwing meat nearby to lure them away.

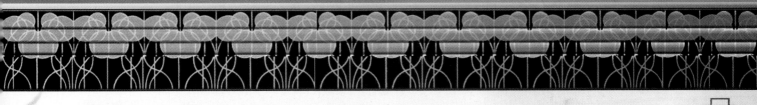

For the fiery path, take a Bone or Spear from a nearby area and light that item with an existing flame; many levels present these, so the hunt is usually a short one. Approach the creatures with the burning implement and thrust it at them repeatedly to scare off the host for a short time. Hurry with whatever Jack is doing, because it's a constant struggle to keep the creatures away from their favorite spot!

The meat route is also easy. Again, take a Bone or Spear, but look for a grub, flying insect, or other such treat. Spike the target on the end of said Bone or Spear, then toss the weapon into a corner somewhere near the creatures. They are more than happy to leave for a considerable time while feasting on the dinner provided to them.

WATER CREATURES

Deeper water on Skull Island is a major threat to anyone taking a bath or swimming along. The "fish" in the water are actually more reptilian in nature and can be quite large. A solid Spear hit or a couple bullets stop them cold, but it's sometimes impossible to fight the enemies because a swimming person isn't able to wield their weapons properly. In those cases, it's often a matter of having a buddy there to cover the swimmer. If the team goes into the

water first, have Jack stay on dry land and snipe any of the waer creatures that come to the surface (the Rifle, thrown Spears, and just about anything else function well enough for this to work because the water creatures are slow-moving and large targets). Then, when the team is safe on the other side of the water, Jack can cross while everyone covers him!

LARGER CREATURES

Larger creatures are found in heavy brush and often appear in somewhat heavy numbers. Though an individual creature is easy to kill, the rush from several such beasts can be quite trying. Distracting hosts of these enemies with food makes them much easier to dispatch. When that is not an option, look for fire nearby and light the grasslands on fire. Areas that have creatures burn easily and the fire frequently clears away some of the creatures directly, then reveals the others at range!

Without cover, it's even easier to pick off the slow crawlers at range.

VENATOSAURUSES

There are three sizes of fast-moving predators on Skull Island, and they function in a very similar fashion. Venatosauruses are made for running across territory and biting their victims to death without mercy or hesitation. It takes an excellent set of battle skills to defeat these enemies, but they offer some of the finest action in the game as a reward.

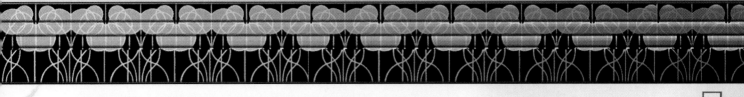

Two bullets or a good Spear throw bring down the small Venatosauruses every time, and they frequently run straight toward their targets, improving the odds that Jack can score the kill before they get to him. The downside is that they come in packs and go after everyone in sight; frequently, that means that Jack has to kill whatever is after him and rush to protect the rest of the team as well. With firearms, that means careful firing, no wasted ammo, and fast reloading during any break in the action. When using a Spear instead, get at least three Venatosaurus kills with a single Spear. Toss at the first, killing it; collect the Spear from the body and plaster the next Venatosaurus. Repeat this until the original Spear shatters, then switch to Jack's projectile weapon or find another Spear.

The larger, green predators of this type (usually appearing one-at-a-time or in small clusters) have more health and a deadlier range of attacks. It doesn't take long for even a single one of these foes to finish anyone off! Luckily, a full hit with a heavy weapon is enough to knock over these predators. Use this knowledge wisely. If Jack gets a flanking attack on one of them, a single Spear can do the trick. Throw the Spear into the enemy, retrieve it while the Venatosaurus recovers, and toss the Spear BACK into it a couple more times. Even if the Spear breaks before the enemy dies, the splintered weapon can be retrieved and used to get a vanquishing blow.

From the front, this technique is more dangerous because it might recover early enough to bite Jack while he is rushing forward for his Spear. In this case, drop Jack's Spear while the enemy is rushing forward; shoot the beast in the face, pick up the Spear, and hurry to the flank for a safer area of attack.

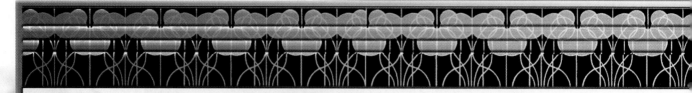

One perk about fighting Venatosauruses is that they are large enough to prohibit their movement in tighter areas but they aren't large enough to break through stone. Have Jack hide in ruins and scrunched areas that the larger ones can't reach. From there, he is able to throw Spears and Bones at his leisure, scoring easy and safe kills without breaking a sweat.

The Blue Venatosauruses are the largest of these three hunters, and they are able to eat almost anything that gets in their way. Frequently, the Blue Venatosauruses attack and slay the smaller ones. These species compete heavily with each other and possess a natural enmity. Luring the two sides into a confrontation makes life much easier for Jack and the team, because it's a given that only one group will survive.

It takes at least four or five good hits to bring down the Blue Venatosauruses. Hide from them in raised areas when possible, or stick-and-move by throwing a Spear/Bone at a charging Blue Venatosaurus and fleeing while it recovers. Use that time to find a new weapon to hurl. Be wary of using smaller stone buildings as shelter when the Blue Venatosauruses are attacking; they are stronger than the Venatosauruses and are able to break through some buildings.

V-REX

V-Rexes are built like the tyrannosauruses of old, and they are even more aggressive about getting their food. Not content to scavenge or like for careful opportunities, these behemoths are the nightmares of Skull Island. Insatiable and carnivorous to a fault, the V-Rexes especially love to eat people and creatures. This offers one of the first defenses against the monsters (shoot creatures in the area to lead the V-Rexes away from the team).

Another way to delay V-Rexes during an attack is to hit them with a Spear or Bone. Though a pinprick, this action annoys them greatly, encouraging them to turn and face whatever has struck them. Remember to have another Spear or Bone at the ready as soon as possible; once

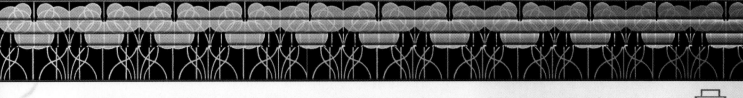

a V-Rex starts chasing anyone, the only way to escape is through a stone barricade or by hitting the beast again with a thrown weapon. These brief delays aren't much comfort, but they are enough to survive.

If a V-Rex is about to strike at Jack and cannot be stopped, turn to face it at the last minute. A V-Rex bite from behind can spell instant death, but an attack from the front simply inflicts a grievous wound.

Don't waste ammunition trying to kill the V-Rexes; Jack doesn't have anything powerful enough to get the job done. Instead, these predators have only one thing to fear on Skull Island, and that is the mighty King Kong.

BRONTOSAURUSES

Brontosauruses are gentle giants on Skull Island. These massive dinosaurs aren't interested in meat, and they especially aren't interested in Jack or the team. The only threat posed by Brontosauruses comes from their heavy, plodding feet. Stay near cliff walls and other natural barriers to avoid falling under a Brontosaurus' shadow. And, when crossing the same area of a herd of brontosauruses, ALWAYS move with traffic; this gives Jack more time to react and prevents him from being caught in the open.

SKULL ISLANDERS

Skull Islanders are humans who have lived on the island for many generations (it is likely that no one knows exactly how long they have been there). These rugged people are not kind or generous, having been shaped by the fierce land they live in, but they deserve either fear or respect. Or both, really.

These humans use thrown weapons and arrows to attack their enemies, and the islanders are deeply aware of the fear that fire causes. Because of this, they use fire heavily in their attack, lighting brush and creatures for maximum effect. To survive these volleys of missile weaponry, stay near walls, avoid open stretches, and hope for the best. When the attacks are made from the cover of brush or wooden structures, return the favor by hurling a burning Spear or Bone back at the natives. This catches their cover and ends the attack.

SMALL LARVE

Though rare, there are Small Larve on Skull Island. These foul things leap onto their targets and try to latch onto exposed flesh. Kong is used to punching his way through the younger generation of these, but the older Small Larve are hardier and require a heavy beating to put down. Kong should enter a fury when he spots the Small Larve, then use charge attacks to knock the creatures about. Once they are dazed, it is easy for Kong to grab the beasts and tear them apart.

GIANT DRAGONFLY

The Giant Dragonflies on Skull Island are quite dangerous because of the diseases they carry. Don't wander too far toward brush or briar patches that are submerged. The only warning before Jack starts taking damage from these flying terrors is that he'll see them start to swarm in the area. This doesn't give him much time to reverse his direction; do so quickly and look for a better path through the swamps.

MASTERING YOUR PART

There are a number of universal strategies that help players make it through the tougher challenges of Skull Island. This chapter explains the methods used in fighting and general survival throughout the game. Also included here are the unlockable extras and tips for achieving higher scores after beating the game.

FIGHTING TO SURVIVE

Many of the challenges on Skull Island revolve around fighting against strange creatures and predators. Without using the best techniques, these fights are considerably harder. Learn how to throw, shoot, and lure enemies into the worst conditions for battle as soon as possible. This is useful for completing the levels in the first place, and it later helps to beat areas with a higher score!

THE UPS AND DOWNS OF FIREARMS

Firearms are extremely responsive for threats of varying size. The larger the threat (in terms of numbers and aggression) the greater the potency of these tools (as opposed to Spears and Bones). As long as ammunition lasts, firearms can be used to dish out heavy damage. The downside of this style of fighting is its duration; nobody on the team has enough ammo to keep firing forever.

Conserve ammo by using Bones and Spears for easier fights, and use the firearms for the dangerous times when they are warranted. If three Venatosauruses jump out of the brush, the sensible path is to launch a Spear into the first and shoot the other two (two taps each with a Pistol/Machine Gun, a bullet per Venatosaurus with a Sniper Rifle, and hope for a double kill with the Shotgun). With more experience, it's possible to use the firearms less and less, but they never go out of use entirely.

Never fire in panic! One of the greatest sources of inaccuracy is the urge to fire immediately when threatened. This is true even within games, when there is no real threat to the player. No matter the size of the creature, remember that Jack is a tough guy who can handle himself. Everything can be defeated, or can at least be escaped. Aim for kills, and don't settle for shots that may hit. Remember that a miss takes more time than proper aiming would have taken in the first place.

WEAPON TABLE

WEAPON	BEST RANGE	PERKS
Pistol	Short/Medium	Large Clips, Easy to Use, Versatile
Shotgun	Short	High Damage When Used Correctly
Sniper Rifle	Long	Scope for Better Zooming, High Damage
Machine Gun	Medium	Large Clips

USING THROWN WEAPONS

Thrown weapons are the hardest to master, but they offer many rewards. First off, an expert with Spears is able to have a high-power weapon in just about every level. Ammo is rarely an issue, these weapons are fairly reusable, and the impact from a good Spear hit rivals a bullet from a Sniper Rifle.

Beyond that, Spear blows carry more stopping power against many targets. The stun effect from damage is not consistent between weapons; Spears are better able to delay rushing enemies, distract V-Rexes, and knock down various targets. Thus, there is a defensive element to Spear use that counters many of the weapon's downsides.

Practice Spear/Bone use with and without zooming. It's important to be able to throw at long range with accuracy or to toss quickly at short range, even if accuracy becomes a bit spotty.

For the long throws, always zoom, and guess high when in doubt (it takes a lofty throw to get serious range). Moving targets are even trickier at range, because leading your target is more difficult; Spears and Bones have a distinct travel time, and that must be accounted for. There aren't any tricks to that. It just takes practice, practice, and more practice.

The short throws absolutely have their place. When Jack is against a metaphoric wall, he sometimes has to put out heavy damage without relying on projectile weapons. Spears and Bones do this decently. Aim for the center of mass, as always, and don't aim nearly as high for these; treat the attacks as direct fire shots at close range. Also master the art of pulling Spears and Bones out of wounded creatures and corpses. Throw these until the weapons break, as there is no reason to waste time or weaponry.

As mentioned before, there are downsides to using Spears and Bones. Though easy on ammo without sacrificing much damage potential, these weapons require higher skill from the user and are slower to bring to bear. The Pistol, Machine Gun, and even the Sniper Rifle are all more responsive to varying enemy threats. Spear/Bone users need to know their levels very well to perform optimally. That way, they can be aiming toward targets early on, without needing as much adjustment before launching the deadly strike.

Another way to minimize the problems of thrown weapons is to abandon them immediately when a situation gets out of hand. The drop weapon command acts very quickly, and Jack can raise his projectile weapon immediately. Carry a good backup weapon (a Pistol or Sniper Rifle, preferably), and switch to that gun as soon as a Spear misses, an enemy recovers too early, or whatever comes out of the blue.

DIRTY TRICKS

At several points in this guide, reusing Spears is mentioned as a brutal way to dispatch groups of smaller enemies (or to grind a single, tougher enemy into dust). Grabbing Spears from the bodies of fallen foes or from recovering creatures is one of several dirty tricks that sets monsters up for a fall.

Another nice trick is to use fire against groups of creatures. If there is a field of grass or briars around a pack of predators, don't hesitate to throw a burning Bone or Spear into their midst. If done from long range, the likelihood of counterattack is minimal. Thus, it's always wise to keep a burning Spear/Bone at the ready when moving deeper into levels, and visually scouting (through the use of zooming), is a fine way to get the feel for a place.

Grubs and other small creatures are useful for distracting creatures. Sure, everyone learns this early on in the game. But, these innocent creatures serve a greater goal as well; they are used to attract predators! Lure Megapedes, Venatosauruses, and various other foes into the open and into a tight pack by throwing a Bone/Spear ahead with a grub or insect stuck on the tip. When all of the nasties gather, tear into them (the Shotgun gains its greatest honors during such times).

Mixed groups of enemies are asking to be exploited. If there is a random creature flying around an area with Venatosauruses or Megapedes, shoot the hapless creature and let the predators gather to feast on it. When a grub isn't available, let your enemies be the ideal substitute!

Kong's battles

Kong's battles have much visual variety and flavor. The underlying tactics to them are not as complex, however; the fights are meant to be fun and epic, rather than intricate and frustrating. The short version is this: use fury when Kong has any break in the action, charge attacks are superb for damage and knocking enemies out of the way, and grapple opponents for the kill as soon as they are knocked down or disabled.

To achieve this, a player only needs to master several tricks. One of them is slapping carefully to knock lesser threats out of the way, or to stop larger creatures from charging themselves. This action is all about timing. Kong can swing quickly enough that it isn't too hard to learn. Watch his range and speed to determine when something is within striking distance. Once they are, give them a smack.

Grabbing smaller enemies is rarely useful unless you are toying with them or have a secondary goal! Throwing enemies into other enemies works extremely well. If that isn't the case, don't waste time making these attacks except for their flash value. It's faster to use charge attacks to bowl through enemies, and time is of the essence; this is doubly true in scored missions for Kong.

OVERCOMING OBSTACLES

Many of the problems on Skull Island stem from barriers that the team has to pass. Some of these are natural obstacles, and others have been put into place by the Skull Islanders.

GRASS

Tall grass grows in many locations on the island; the almost constant rains mixed well

with the beating sun to give everything ample growing opportunities. Though grass won't halt anyone's progress, it slows any of the humans that try to walk through it. Larger predators and even many of the smaller pests don't have this problem. Thus, battling in grassy areas puts the team at a disadvantage. Burn grassy areas to clear the way, or hurry through them as best as possible to fight at higher elevations or at least out in the open.

BRIARS

Briars appear in large thickets, often blocking the way toward critical areas of the level. These cannot be waded through, and Jack even takes damage if he pushes too hard into them. Throw a burning Bone/Spear into the thicket to set the briars aflame, then walk past after the fire dies down.

Moving fire

Blocked areas, due to thicket growth, are impassable without using fire, but sometimes there isn't a burning urn nearby to light everyone's Bones or Spears. That can be quite a problem, because nobody on the team has a lighter or any know how for starting fires on their own. In these levels, Jack has to pass fire from earlier urns to later urns. When the way between the urns is blocked by a waterfall, anything Jack is

carrying will be doused and any fires would be extinguished. To get around this, look for ways to throw Bones or Spears across gaps, through holes in walls and such, to hit the future urns with fire from a distance. This solves the problem nicely.

Opening gates

Gates are opened with turning pillars on Skull Island. Often, there are two of these that need to be used in synch. Look for the levers that attach to these if they aren't already installed in the pillars (the levers are certain to be in the area, and not TOO far away). Bring these back and poke them toward the pillars to install them. Afterward grab one lever and start turning. If there are two levers, a teammate automatically moves to take the other side and help Jack.

Waterways

Like grass, water slows progress and makes it harder to see what is creeping (or swimming) up on the team. When possible, wait for the other folks on the team to move through a waterway while Jack covers them. They'll return the favor when he follows. This is much safer than having everyone go at the same time.

Don't seek a fight while wading around in swamps. Though it's sometimes unavoidable, aiming and dodging are hampered by the poor movement in these areas. Do everything possible to stay on dry land when fighting the fish that live in the water.

Conversely, seek the water when fleeing from creatures that are afraid to cross it. Venatosauruses and their ilk are notorious for being skittish around water on Skull Island. They won't follow Jack in, even if he is fighting them! Use that, and stay safe while making attacks on hydrophobic enemies. Hopefully, the beasts aren't rapid as well.

Wooden bridges

Wooden planks are used to cross the many cliffs and canyons of the island. Put in place at varying times by the Skull Islanders, nobody is quite certain that these "bridges" are going to hold. All of them shake and groan once a person steps onto them, further adding to everyone's concerns.

Fear not! Though it's easily possible to plummet off of the bridges because of a misstep, almost none of the bridges in the game break under Jack's feet. It is almost always safe to take extensive time, walk while looking at the footing ahead of Jack, and make cautious turn on the bridges. Don't overreact, hustle, and pitch over the side.

EXTRAS

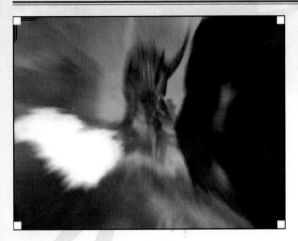 

Completing certain goals in terms of the game's content and high scores unlocks various extra features. View the table below to find out what is in store!

EXTRAS

REQUIREMENT	REWARD
Complete 10% of the Game	Weta Artworks: Environments Part 1
Complete 25% of the Game	Video Mode: Old Movie Filter
Complete 50% of the Game	Weta Artworks: Creatures
Complete 75% of the Game	Weta Artworks: Kong Part 1
Complete 100% of the Game	Video Mode: Horizontal Flip
Score 20,000 Points	Weta Artworks: Kong Part 2
Score 50,000 Points	Weta Artworks: Environments Part 3
Score 75,000 Points	Peter Jackson Interview
Score 100,000 Points	Weta Artworks: Kong Part 3
Score 150,000 Points	Weta Artworks: Kong Part 4
Score 250,000 Points	Alternate Ending

GETTING A HIGH SCORE

After beating the entire game, a new challenge unfolds. Many of the levels are now rated by a scoring system. This gives them extended playability, and people who enjoy getting high scores also are rewarded with extra features (as shown in the area above). This section explains how to improve your scores and also which levels are especially nice for that type of work.

GENERAL IMPROVEMENT TIPS

- Never Waste Bullets
- Use Spears Until They Break
- Slow Down for Jack Levels, for Safety
- Rush Through Kong Levels, for Speed
- Make as Few Attacks With Kong as Possible
- Use Fire, Distractions, and Other Dirty Tricks Frequently
- Be More Aggressive; Kill All Monsters, Don't Let Them Hurt Allies
- Always Get the Killing Blow (Allies' Kills Don't Count Toward Your Score)
- Restart a Level if There Are Any Deaths; For Wonderful Scores, Don't Even Accept Injuries
- Replay All Levels Once Before Trying to Master Specific Levels

Most of the tips above have already been discussed, but a few of them are new and bear mentioning. Scoring in Jack's levels is not based on time. Because injuries are quite damaging to point totals in these levels, it's very useful to slow down, ambush as many enemies as possible, and find the ways to cheaply trash all opponents rather than face them directly.

When Kong is at the helm, it's entirely different. Kong loses huge numbers of points when he dilly dallies, and a high score for him is based off of many kills per swing and getting everything done as soon as possible. Charge attacks wade through enemies without wasting time, and single enemies are not worth the time at all unless their defeat is required.

If the first playthrough, it is suggested that Jack use his teammates to lure enemies out. Once the monsters are chomping on his buddies, Jack is sure to have an easy and accurate shot at the targets. This doesn't work anymore when trying to get a high score; injuries to friends are just as painful as injuries to Jack in this mode. So, take a more aggressive stance when the group is in danger and act assertively to knock everything out of the way. Though accuracy is stressed highly, it's even worth wasting extra ammo if that stops team members from being hurt.

Any death on the team practically demands a restart for that level. Losing 5,000 points in one slice is just too much to bear. Yet, don't go for perfection on day one. Instead, try to make it through each level without a death, and accept the injuries and misses. This builds a large score total very quickly, unlocking the bonus extras without much effort. Afterward, the perfectionists and experts out there can redouble their efforts and try to break their own records!

Note that the scoring system is based around an objective OUTCOME. Many of the levels adjust the scores listed in the table below so that 20,000 points is a good showing for that level, 25,000 or more is a great showing, and so forth. The system is made so that varying levels have a similar outcome, though there are still a number of levels that are specifically easier for quick points.

JACK SCORING SYSTEM

NAME	POINT EFFECT
Chapter Bonus	Varies by Level (Baseline Points)
Big Predators	+5,000
Predators	+1,000
Pests	+500
Bullets Used	-100
Spears/Bones Used	-20
Deaths	-5,000
Injuries	-1,000
Friends Injured	-1,000

KONG SCORING SYSTEM

NAME	POINT EFFECT
Chapter Bonus	Varies by Level (Baseline Points)
Big Predators	+5,000
Pests	+500
Attacks Attempted	-25
Time (Seconds)	-10

LEVEL-BY-LEVEL ADVICE
SKULL ISLAND

SCORE POTENTIAL:	MODEST
TIME TO COMPLETE:	MODEST

The first level of the game doesn't have a big ticket in terms of predators and big predators, and that hurts its total score. Easy to survive, fairly fast to complete, it still makes the list of good levels to try early on. Practice Bone throwing against the Giant Crabs for minor savings on points.

NECROPOLIS

SCORE POTENTIAL:	HIGH
TIME TO COMPLETE:	MODEST

The high number of predators in this relatively easy and short level makes up for the injuries to allies that often occur. It is very easy to score over 20,000 points even in an initial run here. Be extremely aggressive against the Megapedes; they are going after the team and can injure allies without much delay. Better to use Jack's ammo freely and stop that from happening.

SCORPIONS

SCORE POTENTIAL:	MODEST
TIME TO COMPLETE:	MODEST

Scorpions is another easy level in the beginning. With slightly fewer predators, the point total is a tad lower than the Necropolis, but it is easier to avoid injuries. Use fire to destroy the brush in the creatures' area to expose the little critters. Finish the survivors off with Spear throws.

THE WALL

SCORE POTENTIAL:	HIGH
TIME TO COMPLETE:	MODEST

The Wall is a fine investment for points. The extremely high count of pests combine with more predators to allow for a great score. Again, use fire to clear creature areas. Effective use of thrown weapons makes a several-thousand point difference in this level, making The Wall a good place to practice advanced Bone/Spear techniques.

SACRIFICE

SCORE POTENTIAL: MODEST
TIME TO COMPLETE: HIGH

The delay for plot in the early section of the level combined with difficulty avoid archer fire and a difficult fight late in this level make it a somewhat poor choice for the early playthrough, unless you are specifically going through the game again in order. Be especially cautious during the

Venatosaurus/Megapede fight at the end. Stand with Carl and hit the Venatosaurus at close range. Move to the right and grab a new Spear to avoid being bitten retrieving the first, and finish the creature from the flanks.

ON KONG'S TRACKS

SCORE POTENTIAL: POOR
TIME TO COMPLETE: HIGH

The lower rating for kills in this level combined with the high potential for injuries make it a poor choice for early point farming. Enemies are worth half of what they are in many of the other levels, and Jack takes quite a beating unless you are very skilled with fighting creatures using Bones and Spears.

HAYES

SCORE POTENTIAL:	HIGH
TIME TO COMPLETE:	MODEST

Points for kills and penalties for injuries and such are both lowered in this long level. Though it takes great effort to play the level well enough to achieve a high score, the potential is there. Make this run later on, after picking the low-hanging fruit.

Take extra time while fighting Venatosauruses, as they are so good at injuring people. Fight them at range, always approach from the flank, and use the Pistol if needed. Staying in water later on, in Hayes' cavern, is another good way to avoid injury. Venatosauruses are too chicken to get their feet wet. Don't forget it!

V-REX

SCORE POTENTIAL:	HIGH
TIME TO COMPLETE:	MODEST

The wonderful chapter bonus in this level makes up for the trivial number of foes Jack faces. As long as you practice the basics, for bringing down the creatures and avoiding the V-Rex, this level is going to be short and lucrative. Scoring 20,000 points is easy as pie, though getting too much about that isn't possible because of the limited targets.

ANN

SCORE POTENTIAL:	MODEST
TIME TO COMPLETE:	MODEST

This level runs with half of the normal penalties and full kill bonuses. Hurray! The bad news is that this level is heavily dependant on ammunition for the Machine Gun and later the Pistol and Shotgun as well. Those eat into your score, and it isn't entirely easy to fight off the groups of

Venatosauruses without taking a hit here and there. This is one of the finest levels in the game for practicing accuracy with firearms, so that is a major perk!

KONG

SCORE POTENTIAL:	HIGH
TIME TO COMPLETE:	MODEST

Several minutes of work score nearly 20,000 points, and you get to do all of this while playing Kong; that is always a bonus. There is no reason not to grab this level early in the second playthrough. There aren't too many tricks to improving the score, beyond the usual rush to complete Kong levels

quickly. Clusters of creatures are good targets for swipes (a single attack against several of them is good for snagging nearly 1,000 points). They die in droves, and that helps to pay for this level.

THE CANYON

SCORE POTENTIAL:	MODEST
TIME TO COMPLETE:	HIGH

Reduced point values and penalties imply that there are many enemies and bullets in this level, and that ends up being quite true. Jack uses the Pistol against an early flock of creatures, out of necessity (get the first one with a Spear), then takes the Sniper Rifle to the larger flock over the huge

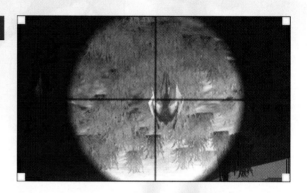

bridge. Play it safe, don't worry about using the Spear heavily, and avoid the dangers of injury and falling off bridges by doing things the sane way. Trying to Spear Jack's way across the great bridge is just asking for trouble.

MEGAPEDES

SCORE POTENTIAL:	MODEST
TIME TO COMPLETE:	HIGH

This is another level with a higher investment that is good for the later round of the second playthrough. Half score for kill and half penalties still rule the day, and there are many chances for allies or Jack to suffer injuries. The fairly large chapter bonus helps out here. Ultimately, there aren't many tricks

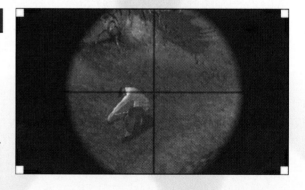

to the level, and a player's final score is HUGELY dependent on the luck and skill of their run. Play Megapedes several times for a major improvement in total points.

BRONTOSAURUS

SCORE POTENTIAL: MODEST
TIME TO COMPLETE: MODEST

The high number of big predators in the Brontosaurus level would be divine for your score even under half points, but they are sadly worth only 1,000 a piece here. That means that it's fairly tough to get a high score from this level, even with VERY skilled Spear use. Using the Shotgun instead means that the potential is even lower.

Luckily, the level is short once you know how to do it, and many of the attacks by Venatosauruses are direct, easy to counter, and both Spears and ammo are in adequate supply for those who are accurate.

JIMMY

SCORE POTENTIAL: LOW
TIME TO COMPLETE: MODEST

This is a good level because it doesn't take very long to complete and it's a great deal of fun. For points, however, there is a rough combination of full penalties and half score for kills. Trying to protect Hayes and Carl from Venatosauruses without using much ammo is a pincer of difficulty, and a single chomp on either of them takes away so much that its hard to get a very high score without several attempts.

ON THE RAFT

SCORE POTENTIAL:	MODEST
TIME TO COMPLETE:	MODEST

This short level is much easier the second time around, when you know what to expect. There aren't too many targets, but their value is full and getting close to 20,000 on this one isn't too hard. On the Raft is a good early investment because of that. Because Bones are inexpensive to throw, they should be used heavily and quickly when trying to prevent injuries. Aggressiveness is very important in this level because the natives are so fast to attack if the brush and bridges aren't on fire.

RAPIDS

SCORE POTENTIAL:	HIGH
TIME TO COMPLETE:	MODEST

The good news is that this level is short and has a high point value! The chapter bonus is high, rewards are at their best, and penalties are halved. Even if you make a mistake and suffer a death, the second playthrough takes practically no time. Getting above 20,000 on this one is EASY, and there is no reason not to go for it. Distract the V-Rexes, as you have to do anyway, and the only other distraction is to hit the creatures early. As long as you can do that, those points are yours.

FIGHT

SCORE POTENTIAL:	VERY HIGH
TIME TO COMPLETE:	MODEST

Even on an initial playthrough, this level
offers point values far above 20,000.
Getting a score of 23,000+ is not hard at all,
especially for a play who enjoys Kong use
and abuses charge attacks. These fast hits
are incredible for taking down the V-Rexes.
Several blows to knock the beasts over, then

a hurried grapple for the kill. You can't go wrong with this level for easy and early points.

SWAMPS

SCORE POTENTIAL:	MODEST
TIME TO COMPLETE:	HIGH

The Swamps require practice to perfect,
as there is fair amount of sniping and
protecting group members here. The
full penalty for injuries complicates that,
making the level easy to complete but
hard to beat with a high score. Best played
later on, the Swamps require expert use of
the Sniper Rifle, especially at medium to
long range.

CHASED BY V-REX

SCORE POTENTIAL: MODEST
TIME TO COMPLETE: MODEST

Though not as rewarding as some of the other Kong levels, Chased by V-Rex still has a reasonably high score without much time spent. The problems that cannot be avoided are the times when Ann is responsible for clearing the way forward. This cannot be hurried, and Kong doesn't get to fight many big predators while he waits. This level is thin on such beasties. Hitting as many of the little foes as possible is the only way to beef the point total. Be doubly aggressive about this while waiting for Ann.

THE SKULL ISLANDERS

SCORE POTENTIAL: HIGH
TIME TO COMPLETE: MODERATE

Time is the BIG enemy in this level. Kong has to spent 100 points for each attack and loses 40 points every second he spends in the area. That is mean, but the extremely high number of villagers that Kong can splatter makes the difference. Don't go after individuals; look for thick packets of meat and charge right down the middle. Think of it like bowling. Try the level two times in a row when you are ready to work on it at all; the difference in time spent is often substantial when the level is fresh in your memory. The second run often yields a very nice score.

TO SAVE ANN

SCORE POTENTIAL:	VERY HIGH
TIME TO COMPLETE:	MODEST

The chapter bonus from this level is practically unparalleled, and you can rake in the points by making a clean run. Avoiding injury and completing the level offers over 24,000 points! The early part of the level is very simply, so the main risk of injury comes during the time when Jack

is waiting for the gate to open. Practice moving between the stone arches to avoid the V-Rex instead of just running AROUND the area and Spearing the predator to delay it. It takes time for the V-Rex to knock down all of the defensive structures, and time is most certainly what you are trying to earn.

VENATOSAURUS

SCORE POTENTIAL:	MODEST
TIME TO COMPLETE:	VERY HIGH

There are many fights in this level (the longest level in the game), and the greatly reduced rewards for big predators hurts what would also be the most lucrative level. Because of the reduced points, it's possible to have a great score here only if you can whether the encounters without wasting

ammo, letting allies get hurt, or being struck down directly. That is all doable, but it takes more practice that the majority of the competing areas. This might be the best one to save for last, quite honestly.

IN THE MUD

SCORE POTENTIAL:	HIGH
TIME TO COMPLETE:	HIGH

Trade weapons with Hayes as soon as possible in this level to avoid losing TONS of points to the Machine Gun; firing at full cost with the Machine Gun means 3,000 points per clip, and there aren't any enemies worthy of that expense here. In fact, the Venatosauruses are basically worthless

(being valued at 250 per kill in this level, when bullets cost 100 points). Let Hayes do as much of the fighting as possible, and only step in for easy kills or ones that prevent an injury. Use Spears as often as possible, especially on the later part of the level, when water creatures are all over the place.

CALL KONG

SCORE POTENTIAL:	HIGH
TIME TO COMPLETE:	MODEST

Welcome to the all-or-nothing level, where points are full and penalties are DOUBLED! If you can make it through without dying or letting Ann get injured or chomped outright, the rewards are wonderful. It's likely that you will need a second try to perfect everything, though. Stay behind the

group in the initial run and push everyone along (if Jack goes in front, it seems to give the V-Rex a better chance to catch up). Then, it's all a matter of shooting accurately at the creatures and distracting the V-Rex as you would normally, with Spears to the rear or face.

KONG TO THE RESCUE

SCORE POTENTIAL:	HIGH
TIME TO COMPLETE:	MODEST

The starting value of the chapter is low, but a huge number of targets wait along the road to glory, and there isn't a high penalty for taking your time. This adds great potential to the level; use Kong fury for efficient victories and learn the level well enough to charge through. With six big predators to fight, there are over 25,000 points in the balance without even considering the creatures.

TO THE PLANE

SCORE POTENTIAL:	MODEST
TIME TO COMPLETE:	MODEST

Greatly reduced point values make this a challenging level for high scores. Avoid using the Machine Gun at all cost, and try to do the level with barely more than Spear use. This is nasty during the Venatosaurus fights. Use cover whenever possible to avoid danger and bottleneck enemies. This is another level that certainly can wait for the tail end of your second playthrough.

TO THE LAIR

SCORE POTENTIAL:	HIGH
TIME TO COMPLETE:	MODEST

With careful sniping and supplementary Spear work, this level is a treasure trove of easy points. The creatures come in very high numbers, so the count of predators is immense, and they are ranked at half value, which is still not too bad for these guys. For single creature attacks, use only Spears. When two are going to come at the same time, snipe one and draw the other into a Spear ambush. Fast and easy points, and an elegant solution as well!

KONG'S LAIR

SCORE POTENTIAL:	LOW
TIME TO COMPLETE:	MODEST

The chapter bonus to too low for this level to be profitable, but it takes almost no time to complete Kong's Lair, so there is no reason not to do it. Use the same techniques that as in the previous level.

FIGHT IN THE LAIR

SCORE POTENTIAL:	VERY HIGH
TIME TO COMPLETE:	LOW

No level in the game offers more points with such a trivial expenditure of time. In two minutes, you can easily pile on almost 30,000 points! The kill rewards are full and it doesn't even matter that there are heavy penalties for time and number of attacks. Destroy as many of the Small Larve as possible while fighting the bigger ones. Those little guys net 400 points a piece even after paying for the swing to smear them.

CHASED BY KONG

SCORE POTENTIAL:	VERY HIGH
TIME TO COMPLETE:	MODEST

As long as you can kill the Venatosauruses from shelter, Jack isn't going to take any injuries, and the rewards for these big predators launch the score for the level. This is another case where a 25,000+ score is doable even on the first try or so. There aren't any special tricks to it either; use the Spears well and make them count. Flank assaults work wonderfully.

HEADING BACK

SCORE POTENTIAL:	HIGH
TIME TO COMPLETE:	MODEST

The game forces you to be point-efficient in these later levels, because there aren't projectile weapons, extra ammo, and so forth. Spear use at the highest tier is essential for the most points, and 22-23K points are available here without too much effort. Follow standard walkthrough procedure for the victory; nothing special is required for a good score.

KONG'S CAPTURE

SCORE POTENTIAL:	MODEST
TIME TO COMPLETE:	MODEST

There aren't big ticket items here, nor is there a very high chapter bonus. However, Kong's Capture is somewhat fast to complete, and there is great fun to be had by stomping all over the Skull Islanders again. As before, look for clumps to achieve the most efficient point totals,

and learn which areas of archers NEED to be attacked for Kong to progress. This cuts down on wasted time, a somewhat substantial point sink in this level (even though the penalties are at their lower values).

IN THE STREETS OF NEW YORK

SCORE POTENTIAL:	MODEST
TIME TO COMPLETE:	MODEST

It doesn't take long to complete the final scored level in the game, and pests are the key to doing as well as possible. Throw cars at distant targets to save time, use charge attacks for anything ahead of Kong, and don't waste effort on anything attacking from the periphery unless there are many foes clumped together.

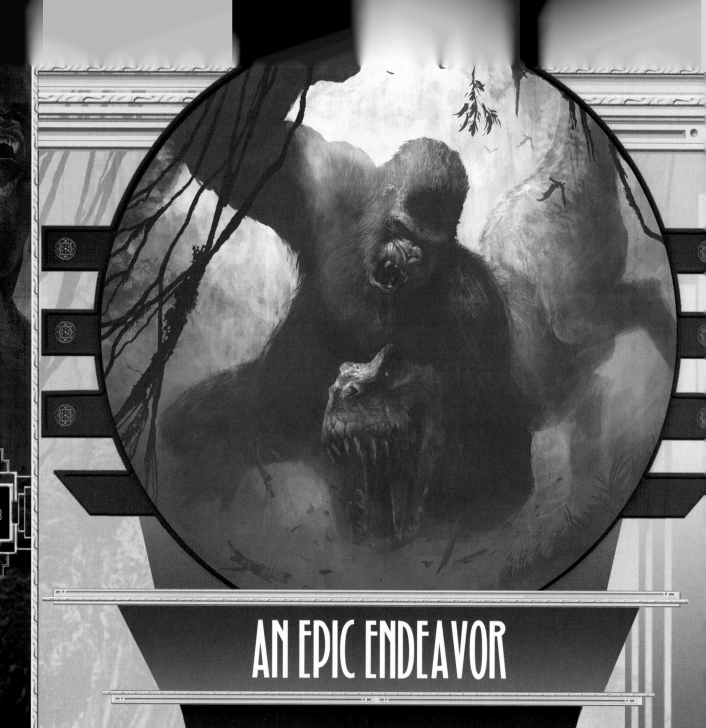

AN EPIC ENDEAVOR

The journey to Skull Island is incredibly dangerous, and everything seems to get more involved and perilous once the team arrives. Without a steady hand, a fleet foot, and a great deal of luck, no one is going to make it through the filming, much less return home with a blockbuster. Most of the burden falls onto Jack for now, and this chapter reveals the safest path through the troubles ahead.

SKULL ISLAND

ARRIVAL ON SKULL ISLAND

You only have partial control over Jack at first. Follow the directions on the screen and get comfortable with your control scheme. The lifeboats are being loaded for a short crossing to the shore of Skull Island, but the waves and rocks of the area are quite ominous. Jack doesn't have any say in whether to stay or go, and his place for now is at the back of the boat. Stay there and wait; it won't be long before the trip ends, one way or another.

Once the team has made landfall, full control of Jack is given to you. Explore the area around the boat and follow the team toward the cave along the rising path when you are ready. Ann has a flare that she stashed for such an occasion, thank goodness, and she lights the way as the team moves into the gloom.

Take the Pistol from Hayes and bring it to bear on the cavern ahead of the party. A series of Giant Crabs attack quite aggressively, though they are bottlenecked to the point where it doesn't take much effort to shoot them before they pose a major threat. Advance into the cavern and keep the Pistol ready; more Giant Crabs could be hidden in the shadows, waiting to pounce.

Reload the Pistol when the Giant Crabs are out of the way and everyone has moved into the cavern with Jack. Smash through the doorway on the far side of the area and exit the caves there. A path leads back down to the sea, and a primitive gateway is at the bottom. Surely this is a sign of intelligent life on the island, but the full extent of this discovery is unclear. Bones are lying on the ground closer to the water (these can be picked up and used as weapons, in a pinch).

SWITCHING WEAPONS

Jack can't carry 20 things at the same time and still fight off the various monsters of the island. Of course, the team is there to help him and themselves! They do this by carrying weapons of their own and using those weapons to fight off whatever comes in their direction.

If Jack needs one of the weapons that another person on the team is using, call to that person and trade weapons with them. As long as the other person is close by, this is fast and straightforward. Otherwise, Jack has to move closer and repeat the process.

Use this to keep Jack from fighting with the wrong weapon for a given purpose.

To open the gateway, walk up to the pillar that stands across from the gateway and use the lever there while Hayes assists Jack. While holding the lever, move forward to turn the pillar; this slowly opens the gate. Carl asks Ann to pose for some quick shots while this is going on, but the take is interrupted by more Giant Crabs.

70

The group of enemies appears by the waterline and skitters up toward the team; use the Pistol to take these smaller foes down while Hayes provides extra firepower of his own. A much larger Giant Crab leaps from the water after the others have fallen, and this one takes many shots to defeat. Get away from the rest of the group to lead the larger one away from Ann and the others. Shoot at the lower part of the creature's body to do damage and avoid its protective shell. While backing away, be careful not to get snagged on anything. The last thing Jack wants it to end up in close range with a gigantic crustacean!

Hayes gets the gate open as the huge beast falls. Hurry back to the group and move with them. The rocky path hugs the cliff, but the footing is good enough to keep from slowing everyone down. Captain Englehorn spots Jack and the others on one of his passes and drops a box of Shotguns and shells in a larger spot along the path. Take these and fight off the Giant Crabs toward the next gateway. With the heavier stopping power of the Shotgun, it isn't hard to break through the wooden barricade and blow apart the cluster of foes.

At the next gateway, pick up the wooden pole on the ground. Use this by the pillar on left and work with Hayes to open that gate. Continue along the path from the other side and follow that until the level concludes.

Getting comfortable in the necropolis

Shortly into the next area, Hayes spots the second boat and yells some encouragement down to them. The current is too strong in the area for the men to land, but the good news is that their boat is intact and they are still strong enough to keep trying.

Move across the rock bridge and stay on the lookout for another weapon crate. It has been logged into the area above the path. Shoot the crate and take the spare Shotgun to replace the one Jack is carrying.

GETTING ANOTHER SHOTGUN

Instead of using the spare Shotgun for extra ammunition, it is possible to switch weapons with Hayes and drop the Pistol for the new Shotgun. This gives the group more total stopping power. Yet, this also means that the meager numbers of shells available to the team are spread thin.

On the other side of the cliffs are walls of burial tombs for the civilization that lives on Skull Island. Considering that there is a flame burning in the center of the valley, it seems fairly likely that these people are still watching over the region. Take one of the Spears near the flame and light the Spear. Using this weapon, poke at the brush on the left side of the valley and clear the way into the tomb beyond.

Carl wants to do more shooting inside the tomb, for "authenticity." Yup, that turns out just as badly as it sounds. Megapedes crawl out of the walls and come at the team from both sides of the room; use the Shotgun at very close range for the best possible damage. Try not to let the Megapedes get onto anyone, and shoot the beasts if they do (they curl around their targets and crush the life out of them). If Jack runs out of ammo, switch weapons with Hayes and keep up the good fight.

More Megapedes burst out of the new tunnel when part of the wall collapses. By now, it's likely that Shotgun shells are running low. If Jack switches to the Pistol, fire about three bullets into each Megapede. Surprisingly, a well-thrown Bone does a decent number on the Megapedes too.

Stay close to Carl during the trip through the tunnels. More of the Megapedes appear, and it's a given that Carl is going to get into trouble with them. Defend him as best as possible.

When the tunnel exits into another valley, look out for the creature that passes over head. Dispense with the Megapedes that make trouble first, then keep a weapon ready for the next creature when it swoops suddenly toward whoever is leading the team. A fast series of bullets is more than enough for this target (two or three good hits are fatal to these creatures).

A FAST VICTORY

If Jack stays at the front of the team while moving out of the tunnel, it isn't too hard to ambush the creature and take it out from behind without worrying about any reprisal!

This has a secondary bonus; the Megapedes rush to feast on the corpse of the beast, and this keeps them from being any threat at all. Dispatch them comfortably.

Cross the decaying wooden bridges on the other side of the valley. Don't move too slowly, as these rotten planks aren't able to carry weight for much time at all. This leaves Jack precariously by himself for a moment, though Ann is brave enough to climb across the gap manually. Watch her as she does this and use the Pistol to blast the series of Megapedes that seek to knock Ann onto the rocks below. Reload between kills, and notice the extra ammunition in the box nearby; it's going to be needed sooner or later.

DON'T SLIP

Most of the edges in the game prevent Jack from falling to his death. This is a kind and gentle feature that gives everyone the chance to explore each vantage point and enjoy the scenery. In this area, however, the bridges are meant to be a challenge, and this normal safeguard is not in place. If Jack slips a bit over the edge while running along the planks, the good times end quickly. Splat!

Take the time to line up Jack's movement across each bridge before stepping forward. This keeps him from spending too much time on the bridges while preventing a deadly spill.

Ann and Jack reunite, and Hayes yells that he and Carl will try to take another route up to the top. Look into the next pass and shoot at the creature as soon as possible. This gives the Megapedes something to eat, making them far less of a threat.

Grab a Spear from the entrance to the pass and light it on the flame ahead. Throw this into the patch of brush by the gateway, then back off to avoid getting singed. Stay near Ann and defend her from more Megapedes that arrive, and she'll climb over to open the gateway afterward. Continue to watch for Megapedes as she makes her climb, then turn to protect Jack from creatures that swoop across the pass.

Another cave offers some shelter from the creatures, but there are large creatures ready to gorge themselves on anyone foolish enough to wade through their masses. Take a Bone from the piles throughout the room, lance a fat grub on the end of it, then throw the Bone off to the side. This distracts the hungry creatures long enough for Jack and Ann to rush through the gap. This completes the level safely!

DEADLY CREATURES

Follow Ann through the dark corridors and stay alert, as always. A creature swoops down through an opening in the roof of the caverns, and two quick shots from the Pistol should save the day. These passages soon break into an open area with stone steps; ascend them to reveal another open pass with a burning flame above and water beyond. Guard Ann as she climbs the rock wall; a group of creatures descend as a trio, but they won't be able to flank Jack when he stays along the cliff wall. Stay focused, as more Megapedes arrive, then run toward the water after Ann destroys the briars that are blocking the way. Swim through the shallow waterway, and have little fear from the creatures that are after Jack. Ann covers Jack very well, using Spears to puncture each foe that breaks the surface of the water. After she helps Jack out of the water, the two enjoy a brief exchange.

Walk through the tiny pass into the next open area. A very sleepy creature is hanging from the rocks in the distance, and there are creatures in the brush. Don't waste ammunition on the creature (it's too far away to hurt badly, and ammo isn't exactly growing on trees around here). Walk through the brush with Ann and fight off the creatures. Shoot the creature after reaching the next fire, then light a Spear to burn away the briars. More creatures approach; they aren't as aggressive as they could be, and it's possible to save ammunition by using Spears instead of the Pistol.

Walk up the far path and pick up the next Spear Jack comes across. Use this at the next briar patch; there is a burning urn above the thicket, and the Spear knocks it off without any problems. This burns down the thicket. Before the smoke clears, the sounds of Hayes and Carl drift from the area ahead. Though comforting to hear and see, Hayes and Carl cannot get across the cliffs in that area, so this is only a temporary meeting. Hayes offers to toss Jack a Sniper Rifle that was dropped by Captain Englehorn. Take this and shoot the Megapedes that are creeping up behind Jack and Ann, then cross the drawbridge to the right.

PASSING THE WALL

Captain Englehorn is close by, but he still isn't willing to land the plane. Perhaps the creatures in this area have given him pause. Use the Sniper Rifle to drop the creature and shoot both of the flames down in the valley (this destroys the two sections of briars that are acting as obstacles), then ambush the remaining creatures while they are feasting. Carry an extra Spear, whenever possible, to get free damage into the fights before spending ammo. The creatures aren't hard to hit, nor are they fast to move in. Retreat and attack if their press ever gets dangerous. There is a box of ammunition in the center of the valley; be sure to take it before leaving.

Use a Spear to skewer the Megapede that ambushes Jack in the connecting path. On the far side is a section that has huge problems with overgrowth. Use the Bone piles as a cheap source of missile weapons to knock down the fires that are on all sides of the temple-like structure. This removes the threat from many of the creatures. Run along the right side, avoiding the foes, and swim across the next gap after Ann has climbed to a higher position. Continue along the only route available and wait for Ann to open the way at the end, where there is a large door. Ann? Aaaaaannnn? Oh dear.

A Golden Sacrifice

The good news is that Jack is fairly intact and that Carl has arrived to lend him a hand. Free from the natives' bonds, Jack needs to find a way to help Ann. Take the path on the right side of the ledge and walk down to the rock bridge below. It won't be long before the natives realize that Jack has made a break for it, and they AREN'T going to be happy about it. Once the game is up, run for it as fast as possible and try to make it to cover without getting hit by the myriad of thrown weapons that follow. Hide beyond the rock boulders for the best cover, and stay with Carl.

When the sounds of the villagers quiet somewhat, take a look around. Carl does a bit of filming, and Jack is free to explore. Look for a tiny crack in the rocks, barely wide enough to pass through, on the left side. Spears and a wider clearing are on the other side. Take the Spears and knock down more fire urns. Keep a Spear armed and also look around the area to note where other Spears are located. This is essential, because a Venatosaurus attacks Carl in the deeper part of the clearing. Several Spear throws are needed to slay such a vicious adversary, and a large Megapede adds to the fray, just to make life difficult. Return to the Spear piles and use the short disorientation period caused by each Spear hit to rearm Jack and prepare another throw.

TAKING COVER

If things get too intense, look for the small, rocky areas where Jack can temporarily hide from the Venatosaurus. It takes time for the enemies to reposition and try to hit Jack when he rushes inside these, and that is often more than enough space to prepare a shot. This is especially good for luring the Megapede to an early death while the Venatosaurus helplessly stands by.

Another good trick with this is to run through the stones and out the far side. This gives the Venatosaurus more distance to cross, because he cannot follow and is forced to go around the stone block.

When the Megapede and Venatosaurus fall, search the clearing for the wooden sticks that fit into the pillars. One stick is inside the stone area, and the other is on the left side of the clearing, stuck in a useless pillar there. Use these on the pillars that flank the gate and then push to open the path. Follow Carl down the rocky ledge on the other side and take a breather at the bottom.

FOLLOWING IN KONG'S FOOTSTEPS

Carl calls for Jack to resume their walk through the rocks and high grass; he says that he heard Ann just a moment ago. Hurry after Carl and don't worry about any enemies for the moment. Something has scared off the inhabitants of the region for the time being. And, after getting to the far side of the grass field, it's clear exactly WHAT did the scaring. Grab a Spear when Carl finally stops and settle in for a fight. After the massive gorilla, called Kong by the villagers, lumbers off, the creatures grow braver. Slip a couple Spears into the larger creature that grabs Carl, then have Jack defend himself against the lesser creatures that attack. Follow Carl's screams down the slope to the right, over the waterfall and toward a wooden gate on the opposite side of the canyon. Pick up and use Spears against the Venatosauruses that race through the grass beyond the barricade.

RECYCLING SPEARS

It is possible to reuse Spears some of the time. The flow of Venatosauruses gets a bit heavy here, and it isn't always safe to turn around and get more weaponry (exposing Jack's rear to a Venatosaurus is just asking for pain). If a Spear is visibly seen sticking out of a fallen Venatosaurus, grab that Spear and use it again!

Also, these Venatosauruses aren't as large or as strong as the one in Jack fought in the previous area. A solid Spear hit against any of these is enough to topple them. That is quite a life saver.

After the Venatosaurus plateau, there is a connecting passage out toward more precarious footing. Use the passage itself as cover while fighting the creatures beyond, and grab the Bones a few feet ahead for more weaponry. When the creatures are out of the way, use the rickety wooden planks to cross the gap. Though these planks moan and protest constantly, they don't break under Jack's feet. Cross slowly and carefully, making extra effort during the turns, and don't worry about the creatures up top (they don't come after Jack until after he gets to the end). That said, rush up the hill on the far side immediately and don't even try to fight the creatures; there are too many to easily best, and they have very nice positioning. Make haste into the cave above and enjoy the relative safety it offers.

Carl and the mother of the creatures are nearby. Walk through the cave and look at the skies on the other side; there are creatures ALL over the place, especially around a nest that the mother is circling. Carl's cries are coming from up there. A box with a Shotgun and some shells is hanging along the path to the right, but two of the creatures need to die before Jack can safely arm himself.

Use Spear that Jack is still carrying or rush for the Bones and Spears up the path. Defeat the two creatures, then break the crate for the much needed Shotgun. Take the precarious walkway up to the top of the nest, and wreak havoc on the children there to clear the way for the big fight. An open box with a Pistol and some ammo is on the left side of the nest from where Jack comes up. Save the Shotgun shells for the big one, and use Bones and the Pistol for clearing the rabble.

To defeat the large flying creature, pick up a Bone or Spear and throw it into it's face when it charges (it is clear that it is preparing a charge because it stops and hovers for a moment). The missile weapons stop the it outright and takes a second to recover; use the Shotgun at this time for close-range attacks that deal substantial damage. Repeat this for two or three passes for a safe victory. When you defeat this creature, Carl is rescued.

Follow Carl back down the path. Don't relax yet; though there aren't many fights left, the remaining creatures by the bridge are going to attack, and there are still a couple Venatosauruses in the grassy area. With Carl's help, it isn't too hard to repel these enemies. Follow Carl all the way back and open the gateway at the end.

A reunion with hayes

Move with Carl through the next area and stay quiet; don't stray too far from him, because there are Venatosauruses in the region. Carl walks past a pillar with some creatures that won't be important until a bit later, and over toward a valley where those Venatosauruses are feeding. Creep toward the shelter on the far side and climb to the top of the structure. Use the window up there as an ambush point and hurl all save one of the Spears into the Venatosauruses. Save the last one for a final assault; light the Spear, leap down, and take close tosses at the second Venatosaurus. Pull the Spear from its body after each hit and repeat the attack! If this fails, retreat to the shelter. There are Bones just outside of the building, and those are useful if the Spears run out.

Also, not that anyone wants to waste the bullets here, but there is a Pistol with several clips of ammunition in a box suspended outside of the building. Knock it down with a Spear tap and collect the goodness.

Two stakes are needed to operate the pillars by the gateway (where the Venatosauruses were feeding). Collect one by taking a grub back to the start of the level, on a Bone or Spear. Toss that near the creatures and steal the stake while they are feeding. Next, light a Spear and stab at the thicket on the left side of the valley (across from the building). Insert these into the pillars and open the way forward.

On the other side of the gateway are crates with a Pistol and a Shotgun. Take the ammo from both crates, regardless of which weapon Jack needs for now. Carry a Spear as well, to save on wasted ammo. There are Megapedes ahead! Fight the lone one in the corridor beyond, then drop into the water when Carl presses forward.

Hurry out of the water onto the small ledge ahead and look to the right (a Megapede comes out from the wall). To be brave and efficient, use the Spear Jack is carrying against it or take the Bones from the pile nearby and throw two of them into the megapede. Repeat this two more times as Jack and Carl advance. When Jack climbs out of the deeper water, onto another ledge at the far end, a final megapede attacks. If the resources are used in the best way possible, no bullets need be spent in this area, but they should absolutely be used as a backup (no need to risk Jack's life needlessly just to conserve on ammo).

Fight through to the next cavern, killing a lone Megapede, then wave to Hayes. He is safe, but trapped behind a rough thicket on the other side of the room. Work around to the left, but don't be hasty. Two Venatosauruses come to watch as Jack crosses the waterfall. Back away, and feel lucky that Venatosauruses are nervous around this much water. From safety, throw at least one Spear into the waiting Venatosauruses, then take the next Spear across once the Venatosauruses get bored and wander off.

Use the smaller stone buildings as cover while advancing through the Venatosauruses' territory, and take any free shots from the doorway to wound the Venatosauruses. It's hard to get the Spear back after a successful hit, but a miss is going to leave the Spear nearby (so this is basically free damage).

Hide in the first two buildings, then make a break for the open area on the right. This heads into water, so there is more safety than it appears. Swim to the stairs nearby, climb out of the water, and quickly head around to the ledge across from Hayes. He'll toss Jack the Machine Gun. Use that to blast the Venatosaurus that is going around, then turn to defend Jack against the Venatosaurus's buddy.

STAY MOVING WHILE INJURED

If one of the Venatosauruses manages to get a bite into Jack, the most important thing is to stay mobile. Only continue an attack if Jack is already facing the Venatosaurus and has a weapon ready to throw. Otherwise, it's much better to make the most of every second and find shelter until the danger period wears off.

Use the fire and a Spear to destroy the thicket below after the fighting is over. Hayes is now free to rejoin the group, though everyone probably needs a change of clothing after that encounter. Sadly, there are two more Venatosauruses on their way. Lure these back toward Hayes and Carl to get extra fire support, then take both of the Venatosauruses out before proceeding. There is a stake on the wall behind the buildings Jack used for cover; take it and open the gateway nearby. Follow the only path out and listen for an interesting new development. Maybe Kong isn't the only game in town.

KING OF THE THUNDER LIZARDS

The rain is intense, and there still isn't any word from other survivors, but a box of Machine Gun ammo is waiting in a crate close by. Take what is there and follow Hayes. Things take another turn then, for better and then for worse. As soon as Hayes calls for a retreat, RUN LIKE MAD! Follow Hayes and Carl toward the next valley, where a gate is barring the path. A creature circles nonchalantly in the air above; shoot it and move behind the stone barrier on the side. There are Spears there. Take one and throw that into the pursuing monster to distract it from Hayes and Carl (who are getting the gate open). Throw a second Spear if there is time, then run to the other side of the valley. Shoot the other creature that appears and move behind another obstacle; yes, there are more Spears there as well. The gateway should be open by now, and it's time to run for it!

DON'T SHOOT V-REX

The V-Rex isn't going to give up in this fight, and it's not worth wasting valuable ammunition on him. Only the creatures are worth the fast kill, to distract the big guy. Otherwise, only use Spears to distract the giant from Hayes and Carl.

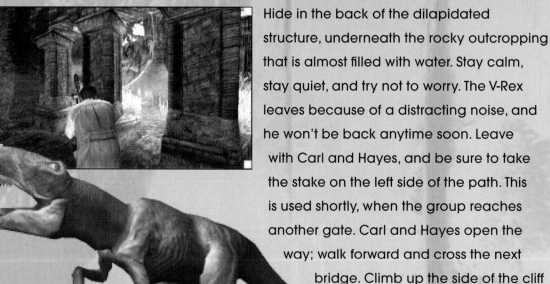

Hide in the back of the dilapidated structure, underneath the rocky outcropping that is almost filled with water. Stay calm, stay quiet, and try not to worry. The V-Rex leaves because of a distracting noise, and he won't be back anytime soon. Leave with Carl and Hayes, and be sure to take the stake on the left side of the path. This is used shortly, when the group reaches another gate. Carl and Hayes open the way; walk forward and cross the next bridge. Climb up the side of the cliff after the bridge fails and press onward. Hayes and Carl try to take the long way around.

Ann's escape

Alone, Jack has to rely on the two friends he
still has nearby, his Machine Gun and his Spear.
Several of these Spears are found along the path,
and a box of Machine Gun ammo is ready to be
knocked down there too. Across a small stream
are several enemies: small Venatosauruses and a
creature. Use the Spears for most of the work, and
rely on the Machine Gun if need be. Jack can
back across the water at any time to confuse the
Venatosauruses.

PROPER USE OF THE MACHINE GUN

*Sure, the Machine Gun was developed to throw a heavy volume of bullets
into an attacking enemy force, but that isn't what it's going to be used for in
this situation. Without heavy supplies of ammunition, the Machine Gun should
be used sparingly. Love every bullet, squeeze the controls for burst fire (two to
three shots at a time), and maximize precision. Do not spray and pray at any
point, even when scared or flustered.*

Many more Venatosauruses rush over the hill, and they come in several waves. There
are enough of these enemies that the Machine Gun comes into play. Try to Spear one
or two from these groups, but take out the middle Venatosauruses with the gun. When
the third group is down, advance and follow a more pleasant sound (the voice of Ann,
who is surprisingly alive). Parallel her movements along the branches and use the
Machine Gun to kill the Venatosauruses that go after her. Before too long, some of the
Venatosauruses wise up and leap over to Jack's area, and creatures come with them.

Shoot the creatures to distract the Venatosauruses, and use the crates of ammo in the area for assistance. The first crate has Pistol ammo, and the next crate has a Shotgun and shells. After the rush on Jack ends, hold still and watch what happens. Don't attack the creatures in the distance; someone else is ready to take care of them.

KONG'S PERSPECTIVE

No more being pushed around by anyone! The primary goal is still to save Ann, but there is a different way of going about things now. Leap from wall to wall and cliff to cliff. King Kong has immense strength and agility, so it isn't hard to do this. Don't worry about any of it, and stick on the big creature the entire time. When the lesser creatures start to swarm, take a swipe or two at them for fast clearing.

The level continues like this for a minute or two, letting players get used to life as King Kong, then the big creature flies up to its nest with Ann. Distract the creature from its prey, then finish climbing onto the plateau. Ann runs off, but the creatures need to die before Kong can happily follow. Use normal swipes against the flocks of lesser creatures, and push Kong into a Fury before attacking the big creature, who comes in for charges here and there. After hitting the big creature a number of times, the command appears to finish it off. The animation for this is splendid, and tapping the controls repeatedly ensures that Kong is successful in doing some of his finest work.

Approach the gateway that is blocked by a fallen pillar and encourage Kong to push the stones out of the way. He can smash through the gate normally when that is done, and follow Ann. A pack of Venatosauruses is on to Ann's scent, so Kong needs to rush and follow her while swatting the pesky dinosaurs out of the way. Charging improves Kong's speed without having any deleterious effects, and it is quite useful here.

After all of the Venatosauruses are out of the way, move to the cliff wall as Ann hurries down a small wooden bridge (that couldn't even dream of supporting Kong's weight). Leap onto the cliff wall and drop back to the plateau where Ann is running. Grab her, just as Kong would an enemy; he'll be MUCH more gentle with her afterward.

DANGER IN THE CANYON

Jack is back on the scene, and the distant drone of an airplane engine gives promise that Captain Englehorn hasn't given up on the team either. Take a Spear while descending along the path and break the crate nearby for more Pistol ammo. The wooden bridge ahead is guarded by several creatures; they won't continue their pursuit for long if Jack backs up, however. The trick is to lure the creatures forward, Spear one, and then retreat. Repeat the process until all are down, or use a few bullets to hurry the action.

After a pleasant walk along the ledges, Jack comes to a larger bridge that has creatures sleeping all around it. Luckily, these critters aren't alert at all. Instead of heading onto the bridge, continue around the bend and look in the crate there for a Sniper Rifle. Use that to eliminate all of the creatures, then take the dropped Pistol back before leaving. Be sure to get all of the creatures (there are a couple on the lower section of the bridge, and there is one flying in the distance as well, so not all of them are in the same spot).

Cross the bridge slowly and move into the wide valley beyond. Hug the wall on the right side for a short time and watch as a massive herd of Brontosauruses migrates past Jack's position. The flow doesn't lighten, so after gathering the nerve, continue. Stay near the right side of the valley and take a Spear from the pile by the next thicket of brush. Turn around and light the Spear with the flame burning not too far away, then climb up the ledges.

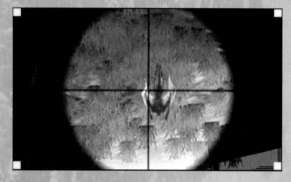

Continue to the rooms across from the grubs and fight the Megapedes using distractions, Spears, and the Rifle (when needed). Caution rules the day here, and progress should be slow. In the connecting area, creatures appear in great numbers. Stay near the front of the area and use grubs and insects to lure these foes into dangerous positions. Attack them with Spears and move quickly to take the most advantage of their feeding times.

Around the corner is a bridge with creatures and another Megapede or two. Toss a Spear off of the bridge with an insect on it to pull the creatures away, then rush carefully for the far end of the bridge. It's easier to escape than to fight the Megapedes, and the level closes when Jack reaches the other side.

LAND OF A THOUSAND MEGAPEDES

Leave the cave and take the Sniper Rifle and ammo while hailing Hayes and Carl. They are on the other side of the large canyon. Stand in place and watch while Hayes and Carl try to leave their ledge; a number of Megapedes attacks, and Jack has to act as a sniper to help out. Shoot at the Megapedes when they gather for each attack; this makes them easier targets. After Hayes and Carl leave, follow the rock ledge and collect a Spear on the way. Snipe the creatures over the wooden bridge later on, then cross safely.

DON'T IGNORE JACK'S BUDDIES

During the sniping events in this level, it is very important to protect the others and keep them from being overwhelmed. Take too long making a shot or try and go ahead without helping and the game will end.

There is more Sniper Rifle ammo on the far side of the bridge. Stay there and help to defend Carl and Hayes. Stay ahead of the game by keeping Hayes from being injured; if he takes a heavy knock from the Megapedes, he won't be able to defend himself afterward (forcing Jack to use more ammo). Giant Crabs slip under the door during the attack, and they too must be destroyed.

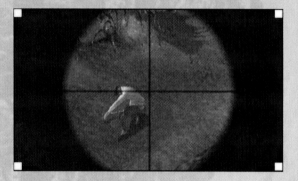 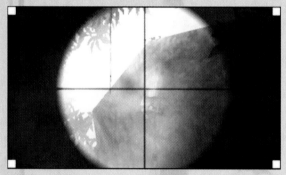

Finish crossing the bridge and follow the path forward, hopping down into a shaded area. Creep forward and snipe the creatures around the turn to distract the Megapedes below; use that time to obliterate the rest of the Megapede group. A Pistol and more ammunition are found near the barricade on the opposite side of the yard, and more Megapedes lurk in the waters past this position. Use several more shots from Jack's Rifle to kill the Megapedes. Retreat to the steps on the higher section of the area and look up; there is a burning fire way above. Shoot that urn with the Sniper Rifle; it lands on a stone basic below and the fire continues. Light a Spear in that basin and toss it through the opening on the left side of the cave to light a second basin.

Use the Pistol for anything that remains in the cave and follow the path toward a larger chamber, where Jack meets Hayes and Carl again. Fight the Giant Crabs there before descending, and take more Sniper Rifle ammo from the crate near the top. When all of the enemies are dealt with, return and get a burning Spear from the second basin. Light the thicket at the top of the last room and collect the necessary stake when the fire burns out. Use this to open the next gate.

Don't stand under brontosauruses

Jack is back in the long canyon. More of the Brontosauruses are wandering through, and there are both large and small Venatosauruses skulking about as well. Move with the traffic, as it were, and use the sides of the canyon as resting spots to watch for large feet and approaching danger from the ground. Switch back and forth from each side to avoid the smaller thickets that block the way. The first time the path is totally blocked by a massive thicket, take the ledge on the right to skip past.

The second time the path is fully blocked, look for a burning fire on the side of the canyon. Slip around a small waterfall there and use the ledge beside the basin to attack the large Venatosauruses and set the thickets on fire. Throw lit Bones from a pile beneath the ledge for the brush itself and save the better Spears for active targets.

WET WEEDS DON'T BURN

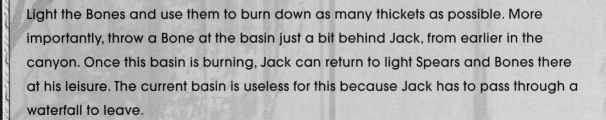

> Submerged thickets can't be burned. There are several of these in this part of the canyon. Even worse, those briars are likely to hurt Jack seriously if he wades into the water and touches them.

Light the Bones and use them to burn down as many thickets as possible. More importantly, throw a Bone at the basin just a bit behind Jack, from earlier in the canyon. Once this basin is burning, Jack can return to light Spears and Bones there at his leisure. The current basin is useless for this because Jack has to pass through a waterfall to leave.

Light another Spear or Bone at the next basin and start running. There are too many Venatosauruses to fight comfortably, Jack's ammo won't hold out, and the danger is too high. Beyond that, it's going to be a dangerous run back through the canyon anyway. The peaceful Brontosauruses are a bit anxious, and the resounding cries of a greater predator explain their change. Run fast, stay near the cliff walls to avoid being squished, and get back to Carl and Hayes. Light the thicket that was blocking the way initially and move into the safety of the pass beyond as soon as the heat subsides.

Lending Jimmy a Hand

This level is filled with carnage. While heading down toward the river valley, Jack and the others are going to meet waves of Venatosauruses and creatures. Most of these targets are going to be soft enough for fast kills, so long as the Sniper Rifle is used effectively and Spears are kept at the ready.

Stay close to the others and let their weaponry supplement Jack's actions. When the Venatosaurus rushes get a bit intense, pull away slightly; the Venatosauruses often go for Jack either way, and this gives Hayes more time to shoot. Take down creatures at longer range to avoid their attacks AND to provide a distraction. There are also insects buzzing about that can be skewered and used as bait.

Around the lower portion of the valley is a warm sight; Jimmy is still fighting the good fight. Use the Sniper Rifle to support him, and Hayes is likely to do a good job protecting Jack's flank while this happens. Jimmy hops onto a simple raft once the next wave of Venatosauruses fails to have dinner with him, and he sails to safety (hopefully).

Take the path that flanks the river and stop once the group reaches the next gate. Some of the locals have prepared a trap for Jack, and a large pack of Venatosauruses charges into the field once the gate opens. Stay near the back of the area, with the others, and use the Rifle and Bones to fight off the group. Don't bother trying to save ammo; this is a battle that can easily turn sour. Any time that the Bones aren't doing the trick, let loose with a clip of Rifle shots to thin the herd.

When that ambush fails, the natives start firing arrows at the group; this continues for the rest of the level, so stay near walls and avoid being out in the open for long periods of time. Stop when the group reaches various thickets and wait for the villagers to burn the way clear. Even though this isn't what Jack's enemies are trying to accomplish, it works well either way. A few more Venatosauruses attack on the far bank of the river, after the team crosses a fallen tree. That is where Jimmy has beached the rafts. Hop on and wait for the current to pull the team out of there.

On the raft

Jack and Jimmy are on the rear raft while Carl and Hayes are take the front, but things don't stay simple for too long. There are Megapedes in and around the water, some creatures too, and the river sadly flows directly through native territory. Not safe at all.

One perk is that Jack's raft has a full supply of Bones to throw. If all of the ammunition is depleted, these are mana from the heavens and should be used constantly to attack the Megapedes as soon as possible. Zooming in for higher accuracy is often a substantial bonus here, when dodging isn't much of an issue (there just isn't enough room to move around even when dodging would be a good idea).

Approaching the villagers' area, the danger increases greatly. There are often one or two enemy archers on the banks or above the river, on bridges. To keep these groups from destroying the team, turn their fire back on them! Grab the Spears they throw or simply light the Bones on the raft and hurl these into the bushes surrounding the banks and bridges. The resulting fires keep the archers at bay, preventing their deadly onslaught.

THROWING AT LONG RANGE

Not only is it a good idea to zoom in before throwing Spears and Bones at the bushes ahead, but it is very important to aim way higher than normal to account for the distance. This isn't too hard to master, but when in doubt, always aim high.

With the worst of the village bypassed, the rafts are forced through rapids and over a bit of a fall. Hang on and hope for the best.

NAVIGATING THE RAPIDS

Perhaps it was a bit early to assume that the worst was over. Though most of the beasts in the area have trailed off, there are still two large carnivores on the team's rear. Both are V-Rexes, and they are hunting as a team. This is a challenging section, and it takes careful throwing, turning, and timing to make it work out in Jack's favor.

First, face the river behind the raft. From that angle, the first V-Rex will be on the left, and its partner will be on the other side of the river. Use the infinite supply of Bones on the raft to resupply and hit the V-Rexes each time they come closer. The first test is from the V-Rex on the left side; hit it with a Bone during its approach, and slam it a couple more times as it yells and makes another pass.

FACING A V-REX

Jack loses his life instantly if he ISN'T facing a V-Rex when it attacks. Yet, if he is watching and is struck from the front, he'll survive (barely). Thus, it is always important to keep one or both of the V-Rexes in front of Jack.

The second V-Rex follows from the other side and is somewhat less aggressive; this one is more of a distraction throughout the river race. Toss Bones toward it when it comes near, but don't spend much time aiming for it and trying to reposition, else the left V-Rex is likely to get a killing blow in from behind.

Complicating matters, there is a creature that swoops in on the raft after the second V-Rex is warded off. While the V-Rexes are rushing the flanks for a better attack, this creature comes down behind Jack's raft. Hit it with two Bone throws, though the first might be enough to knock the creature into a V-Rex's waiting mouth, and that is more than enough to do the trick.

After the next dip in the river, two more creatures attack in a similar fashion. This is a tricky moment because both go after Jack. Throw as quickly as possible with the Bones; the enemies are close enough that hitting them is very easy. Save Jack through pure aggressive actions, because dodging is still impossible.

Next, the V-Rexes make a final bid for the rafts. Use a stray shot or two to slow the V-Rex on the right side, but look overhead to its buddy on the left (this one cleverly advances past the rafts and tries to cherry pick Jack on his way past). Distract him with Bones, duck, and know that it isn't far until the rafts enter a covered section of the river. Even if one of the V-Rexes makes it to the other side first, something has to go right sooner or later.

A GRUELING FIGHT

King Kong is ready to be a hero again. Stop the V-Rex from getting to Ann. Put Ann down first, even if that means getting nudged a bit by the V-Rex, then unload on it once Ann is safely out of harm's way.

Don't try to push Kong into a Fury; the V-Rex is too aggressive to allow that, and it frequently interrupts Kong with a nasty bite. Use charge, and attack while positioning the V-Rex near one of the walls. Follow by grabbing and throwing the monster into a cliff so that Kong can beat it savagely from behind. These attacks knock V-Rexes down easily, and that is when they are most exposed.

If the V-Rex grapples with Kong and tries to bite his head off, press the controls quickly to shake the dinosaur away. Once Kong gets the upper edge and grapples with the wounded V-Rex, a similar struggle occurs, though this time the V-Rex ends up with a bit of an overbite.

Ann has made it quite a distance during this fight, and she still needs help. Lift the pillar by the nearby gate, then smash through. Jump along the vines and cliffs, and don't let the Venatosauruses in the way stop Kong. Pick one up and hurl it into the next gateway to create an opening while having a good time.

Several jumps later, Kong lands near the two V-Rexes that are hunting Ann. Go into a fury before the V-Rexes know what is about to hit them, then make a series of charge attacks to deal wicked damage to the beasts. Rip the jaw off of the first V-Rex, then break the next one in like fashion (though with a different animation that looks wonderful).

A SHORT BREATHER

If Kong is taking too much damage, he is able to hop back up to the cliffs and swing there while catching his breath. Although Ann shouldn't be left in danger for too long, this is a good way to get the V-Rexes off of Kong when he can't quite build momentum in the battle.

At any point, it's possible for either of the V-Rexes to wander off and look for Ann. When that happens, she'll scream her head off to let people know that she is in serious trouble. Slap the offending V-Rex around to dissuade the beast. It's much better to have the dinosaurs munching on Kong than Ann; the big guy take slightly more punishment.

THE SWAMPS

Finally, Jack gets a reprieve on his lack of ammo. A crate with Pistol ammo is in front of the team's camp, and burning the nearby thicket reveals a crate with Sniper Rifle bullets as well. Take both of these and decide which weapon to carry into the area. The Sniper Rifle is a very good choice, but either serves nicely.

Cover Hayes and the team as they crawl through the mud and deeper water. There are water creatures in the gloom, and those things take modest damage to kill. The first encounter with the fish is light, but the pond that has to be crossed soon afterward has many of the blighters. Wait until the others have gotten across and can cover Jack before following them.

Over in the next section of swamp, there are more fish and a creature overhead. Shoot the creature out of the sky and let the fish converge on its body. Kill them there with Hayes assisting in the attack. Reuse the Bones in the swamp when possible, and cross very slowly to give Hayes the most time to set up his attacks. More Sniper Rifle ammo is waiting at the next dry spot, so a few bullets here and there won't set the team back.

MALARIA? HEH, THAT IS NOTHING

There were a few small spots with Giant Dragonflies in the Canyon levels, but here there are several nasty patches of grass and brambles with the biting insects. Jack can certainly be killed by these creatures, especially if he is backing away from fish or other attackers. Stay wary and reverse Jack's steps immediately if the screen begins to fill with Giant Dragonflies.

Use those extra bullets on the creatures that are hanging from the branches above the path. There are three of them, and they attack in unison if anyone gets too close. To keep Hayes safe and sound, it's better to snipe the creatures before they take flight.

The last trouble in the level comes in the form of a thicket near another body of water. Shoot the creature that is circling the flames above, then climb up the narrow stone wall and use that flame on one of the Spears up there. Throw that into the thicket below to clear the way for the team, and defend Jack from another creature that appears. Hayes shoots from the ground to help out, making the second foe quite easy.

Stay on top of the stone structure and fire at the many water creatures as they come out to attack the team. Wait until just after each fish attacks for the easiest shot at them; they stay in place while biting their targets and worrying them. It takes a number of shots to ensure a safe crossing, but Hayes returns the favor well when Jack makes his swim. Dodge a bit from left to right while moving forward in the water; plenty more fish are after Jack, and the motion helps to keep them from pinning him.

Climb the stairs on the other side of the swamp to achieve some measure of dryness.

CHASED BY A KING

By this point, Ann seems to realize at least to some extent that Kong is a heck of a lot better than the villagers, dinosaurs, and odd beasts that inhabit the islands, so she doesn't run away from the big guy much at all. In this level, she's even a critical part of his ability to make it through the region. A beautiful pair, if ever there was one!

To start the level, swat the Venatosauruses and creatures that are inbound, then pick Ann back up and carry her to the top of the pillar in the middle of the plateau. Ann uses her flaming Spear to destroy the brush at the top of the cliff, giving Kong the chance to climb up. Do so, and pick up Ann as she rushes along the waterfall above.

Knock aside any of the minor threats to the couple as Kong leaps through the jungle. Everything is carefree until Kong climbs another ledge and is again stuck with a wooden barricade over his head. In this case, Ann needs some open flame to light her Spear. Destroy the gate on that plateau and kill the Venatosauruses inside before they get a chance to hurt Ann. Pick her back up and climb the pillar there before releasing her. Helpfully, she destroys the brush and barricades a second time. Wait for the debris to fall before climbing up, and fight all of the creatures that attack to pass this section.

Chase after Ann, who has dinosaur and trust issues, and leap along the right path. As she is fending off a V-Rex of her own, Kong must break through a blocked gate. Ignore the Venatosauruses in the way and push the pillar… ouch, one moment on that. Another V-Rex is on the move, and that needs to be dealt with immediately. Have Kong slap the V-Rex with a heavy charge attack, then throw the monster into the wall nearby. Stay aggressive and continue doing this until Kong can get a grapple against the dying creature and end its assault.

Push the pillar of stone out of the way, then break through the wooden gateway behind it. Ann doesn't have much time left, but Kong should be there for her!

IT'S AS EASY AS…

This tiny level is a story section that develops what happens with the team after Hayes perforates Kong's back with the Machine Gun. There is a frightening incident with an angry, GIGANTIC gorilla that follows. After that, Jack listens to Carl, who is despondent about damage to his camera. Hayes and Jimmy are far more focused on saving Ann

and getting off of Skull Island. As Jack runs off to see what can be done about those things, control switches back to Kong.

ROUTING THE SKULL ISLANDERS

The battle resumes as Kong is being attacked by the villagers. There are two groups of archers above the gateway behind Kong, and Venatosauruses are approaching to munch on Ann. Use the Venatosauruses efficiently by throwing them AT the archers above. Once the archers are down, Kong can stop dodging about and focus on the main gateway. Lift the pillar in front of it and smash the gate to pieces. Pick up Ann and move out.

A glorious rampage of carnage ensues as Kong tramples a city and dozens of the violent natives. Swat, punch, and enjoy the rush of power as Kong cuts a swath through the place. After jumping over to a far plateau, Kong is stopped by another barricade. As before, Ann is deployed to solve the dilemma; it's going to take her the better part of a minute to do this, however. Have Kong smash every native that leaves the three caves along the cliff wall, and throw the first thing that he can grab when a creature tries to carry Ann away. After that, she'll light the barricade.

Climb up and take the lovely Ann again, then leap from branch to branch until Kong finds the next gateway. Try to exit there.

Saving ann

Hurry to the front of the cave as Jack and look at the developing problem. Ann has quite a pursuer, and Jack doesn't even have a weapon to distract the hungry V-Rex on her tail. Rush along the path to the left and try not to think about what Jack is actually doing. When the V-Rex corners her in a thicket, run under the creature's legs and look for the small pile of Spears on the other side. Toss one into the V-Rex's face and ditch immediately. Run under the stone arches along the river and take another Spear from the piles in the yard there.

Switch between using the Spears to slow the V-Rex once he comes through and hiding among the stone arches for temporary protection (VERY temporary, as the V-Rex is fully capable of knocking the stones over). Stay on the opposite side of the stones to give the monster a slower time getting to Jack. Ann climbs onto the area above and opens the door. Don't break position until she yells that she's done it.

Hurry through the door and up the path by the cliff. Walk to the top of the section that Ann is climbing and Jack will automatically bend over to help her finish the trip. From there, it's a quick journey back into the crags, where Hayes and Jimmy are waiting. A happy reunion.

The cave

Follow Ann and the others through the stony passages and don't be too scared when Kong pokes his arms and head into the area. He isn't trying to hurt anyone (at the moment), and Ann explains that he wouldn't harm her or any of her friends. It's good to hear, though it might be a tad hard to swallow. She climbs up to speak with him

directly; proceed along the watery base of the tunnel and meet Ann at the end. Say hello to Kong.

Finding a venatosaurus

A large, open cavern threatens the team with its presence in the next level. Run to the top of it as the sounds of Venatosauruses fill the area, and take cover inside the stone ruins. There are Bones, Spears, and two crates there. A Sniper Rifle and a Shotgun are available for the group. Take the Shotgun and let Hayes have the Sniper Rifle. Cover the group from the ruins and shoot at the Venatosauruses that try to move into the area. Don't be shy about blowing ammunition in this fight (the Venatosauruses are tough, and these aren't creatures that go down from a single Spear hit anyway).

When the major wave of Venatosauruses have fallen, a HUGE Venatosaurus attacks and starts to eat some of the other ones. Kill the Venatosauruses on the periphery and let the big guy do what harm he will. Don't antagonize him until he is done with the others; at that time, blast into the blue one at close range with the Shotgun. Several shots made while the rest of the group attacks as well should finish him.

With the central area temporarily cleared, escort Ann down the left side of the room and into a side tunnel. She is looking for both fire (to destroy the growth in front of the exit) and for a stake to operate the mechanism. Take a Bone or Spear, and kill the Megapedes along the way. There are Giant Crabs in the room at the end of the passage, where a burning fire roars. Fight the Giant Crabs with the Bones in that room; they are too slow to offer a major threat. Then, throw a burning Bone up at the basin on the ledge.

REVERSE THE ORDER

It doesn't matter which tunnel Jack explores first. It's possible to grab the lever for the pillars before getting the fire.

Return to the ledge and use the Spears in that area to clear the previous room a second time (there are Giant Crabs there now, and more Megapedes). Light a Spear when the enemies are dead and carefully travel back to the team. Light the thicket and travel to the other side tunnel in search of a lever to use. Many Spears sit at the entrance to that tunnel; these are needed to hit the Megapedes and Venatosaurus that start fighting each other at far end of the corridor.

The next small room has a burning fire and is filled with sounds from below. Use the Spears next to the fire and attack the Venatosauruses and Megapedes in the grasses beyond. Take the lever from the pillar there and return to the central area. With the thickets burned and the lever installed, the team opens the gateway and is able to leave.

BURNING FOR VICTORY

Light the Spears and throw them into the monsters as they fight in the grass. This catches the area on fire and slays even more of the enemies. Do this with both major patches of grass to clear the room in more ways than one.

DOWN IN THE MUD

Carry a Spear from the previous level, if possible, and use that to fight the smaller Venatosauruses in the next valley. Only two come at first, but more follow shortly. Use the time in between to grab the Machine Gun from a broken crate along the path. Shoot the Venatosauruses during their advance, switch back to the Shotgun, then continue.

Use a Spear from the left fork in the path and kill at least one of the creatures over there. Return to the team and snag an insect along the way. Use this to distract the creatures down the right fork, where everyone is trying to walk.

Take another Spear from the flame near the spiders and return to burn the thicket beside the team.

CREATURES DON'T LIKE FIRE

It doesn't often come up, but creatures can be chased away from areas by fire if Jack doesn't have any bait to lure them away. If they creep back to their area when he is getting the flaming Spear, use the threat of immolation to distract them when returning to the group.

Follow the route past the thicket, and Spear the minor number of water creatures that nibble at the team as they make progress through the swamp. Captain Englehorn is flying above, and it is possible that he is aware of the team's position.

Climb onto the ziggurat that is covered with briars and Spears. Creatures with one of their big creatures attack, and everyone needs to work together to fend this one off. There isn't much room to dodge, so the priority should be to knock as many of the little creatures down as possible, and quickly. Use the Shotgun for any early rushes, then sit back for simple Spear use. Once the fight is down to the big creature and its trailing creatures, there isn't enough damage potential for the enemies to take anyone out (they swoop and can wound people, but recovery is likely before the next attack, especially if Jack goes onto the offensive with the Spears while the enemies are trying to hover).

Follow Hayes as he heads down the ziggurat on the other side. Keep a Spear ready and don't get ahead of anyone; several water creatures attack the group from the front and rear, so it's useful to have a good view of the entire scene. Defeat these before worrying about the small Venatosauruses ahead (they won't come into the water). As such, these foes are easily dispatched with the Spears that are conveniently left by the water's edge. A box of Sniper Rifle ammunition is luckily waiting on the dry area. Take that!

Carry a good Spear across the swamp and into a series of blocked, submerged tunnels. Fish are everywhere, and they attack most often in pairs. Use Spears carefully in close quarters for fast kills. Throw, kill, retrieve, and throw again. This is actually better than bothering with the Rifle, as the water creatures are extremely easy to hit and die from a single Spear toss.

Maneuver to the back of the submerged area and to the right side of it. There are steps leading up from there.

Call to Kong

Captain Englehorn is coming around for a water landing, and there is a perfect spot not even a quarter mile from the team. Move forward with the others and keep a peeled eye for signs of any trouble. The Captain makes a textbook landing, and his subsequent actions are even more impressive. Good reflexes pay for themselves when you're a pilot!

Follow the others and race up the path on the left. Don't look back, turn around, or bother to slow the pursuing V-Rex. Even when Hayes tells Jack to slow him down, choose the SANE decision and keep running. In the next valley, Ann develops a plan to stop the monster, but the dinosaur breaks through a side area before she can put it into motion. Hide on the right side of the field, under an archway where Hayes and Jimmy huddle. Throw Spears at the V-Rex to distract him, then follow Ann up a side staircase to escape once the V-Rex begins to break through.

Jack's duty is to shoot the creatures and use them as bait while Ann climbs the rock face. Throwing Bones into the V-Rex's rump offers brief respite for Ann as well, but creature sniping is far more effective. Some of the creatures even attack Ann directly; they are obviously the best targets of all.

Once Ann lights the signal fires, help arrives. Bad news for Mr. Chewy.

KONG TO THE RESCUE

Kong is here to save the day! Battle the V-Rex as Ann throws Spears into its neck and body. This fight is much like the earlier battles with these great lizards, so Kong shouldn't have a problem. The challenge is to get Ann back after a big creature steals her away. Hurry toward the gateway, throw the pillar aside, then make a charging attack to break the gate open while making progress (there isn't much time before the big creature eats Ann, so this haste is required).

Jump and run through the area, then stop to swat the larger groups of creatures while climbing. They tend to pile onto Kong and pull him off of the wall. If that happens, tap the controls quickly to get the host off of Kong.

Another leap through the jungle, and soon Kong is ready to fight two big creatures and their horde of children. When the big creatures retreat for their slower attacks, send Kong into a fury. After that, swats and charge attacks do brutal things to the comparatively fragile big creature, and Kong doesn't need many hits to put them down. It's likely to take two doses of Kong Fury to finish the match, but creatures aren't nearly as good at interrupting Kong as the V-Rexes are, so the investment is worthwhile.

Climb up the pillar after the creatures are dead and clear the way for Ann. Move the pillar, trash the gate, and carry the lovely Ann out of the area. There are several jumps ahead that are more challenging and complex than usual (often, it's just a matter of pushing Kong forward and leaping to his heart's content). Here, however, there is lava to contend with. Leap over the branches onto the vines over the lava, then let Kong slip down a tad. Jump from there onto the central pillar and push to the right to have Kong switch sides; once he is on the other side of the pillar, leap again and climb away from the lake of fire.

Two more V-Rex are rearing for a fight with Kong across the next valley. Put Ann down to free Kong's hands, then lay into these fiends. Attacks that cover a large area, such as Kong's charge attack, are fruitful. If Kong is in trouble, jump from side to side in the valley using the tree by the waterfall. Once the second V-Rex falls, send Kong into a fury and then deal with the third V-Rex that arrives (bad for him to be alone and facing a furious Kong). A series of charged attacks finishes the fight before it even starts.

Open the last gateway, and Ann can rest a bit easier once again.

TO THE PLANE

Jimmy is pretty emotional from the strain of constant fighting and fear, and he charges away from Jack at the beginning of the level. Before long, two of the larger Venatosauruses are on top of him. Stay back, with the modest shelter, and toss Spears to distract the first Venatosaurus. Kill that one while Jimmy tussles with the other, then move to help Jimmy as soon as the incoming Venatosaurus falls.

Move to the side of the valley and open the gateway there. Englehorn is flying not too far away, still vigilant and ready to land if he gets the chance. On the other side of the passage is the valley where the team entered the area (being chased by the last V-Rex). More Venatosauruses have moved in, and creatures are feasting on the remains from some of the kills that have been made. Break through into cover at a small building on the right side, and use that for safety while ambushing the Venatosauruses. There are Spears nearby for ammo conservation.

Continue moving down the valley and fighting the creatures with Spears. Jimmy helps a bit, luckily. Light a Spear in the next hut on the right side, then toss the Spear into the central thicket. Take shelter in the next building beyond, as more Venatosauruses are on their way. Kill the first Venatosaurus that meanders on by with a Spear, taking the original Spear out of its body and repeating the toss several times. Break the ammo crate next to the building and use the Machine Gun inside to trash the other Venatosauruses and creatures that come to investigate.

After that fight, take the Rifle back if Jack has a great deal of ammo for it, and use the next fire hut to light the rest of the thickets blocking the path toward Englehorn, who has landed and is ready to pick up Jimmy.

Reaching the lair

There is a great deal of sniping to do in this level. Smash the crate where Jack starts, collect more Sniper Rifle ammunition, and move out to the waterfall. Stop there and shoot the three creatures that are flying off in the distance (the third one won't be easily spotted until the first two are down). Then, make a slow climb up the stairs in front of Jack, stopping at each tier to shoot the creatures that come forward and look for future threats off in the distance. Take them all out now to save Jack as much trouble as possible.

Break through the wooden barricade at the top of the stairs and walk into the tunnels. The area on the other side of the corridor has Blue Venatosauruses that are way too large to fight comfortably. One of them comes initially, but a second appears after the first is dead. Creatures cover the higher ledges as well, so safety is at a minimum. For a victory without too much trouble, climb the first stairs and use almost all of the Spears there to wound the Blue Venatosaurus. Then, rush to the barricade on the right side of the area and break through it as quickly as possible, before the predator can smash its way in behind Jack. Use the last Spear from earlier against the creatures that come down, and shoot with Jack's Rifle to finish either of them off.

Repeat the Spearing from the higher tier, where the Blue Venatosauruses cannot harm Jack. When the weapons run out, rush to the opposite side of the area while the blue one isn't looking, and break through another barricade. Finish the second Blue Venatosaurus from up there, then use the last Spear from that position to light the thicket across the way. Snipe the creature that is feeding up there, and take either a grub from the front ledge or a burning Spear to chase away the spiders that are guarding a lever at the to of the far ledge. Bring the lever back to the front and use that to open the gate.

Take the Shotgun shells from the crate beyond, but switch back to the Sniper Rifle unless Jack has a large stash of shells already. Smash through the barricade on the right and pass through there.

INSIDE KONG'S LAIR

Use the crate filled to the breaking point with more Sniper Rifle ammo as a sign and get ready to shoot more creatures. Turn the corner and look up the next set of stairs toward the rocks above. There are MANY creatures in the way. Keep a trusty Spear nearby, to fend off any of the creatures that come down to investigate, but use the Rifle to kill the vast majority of the creatures before climbing. Enter the rocks at the top and move all the way through that area without fear; all of the monsters and beasts up there have been scared off by something. When Jack reaches the other side, he'll find out what (and this time it's a good thing).

Swim past the rocks and out toward Ann. Talk to her and find out how things have been. Kong is taking a bit of a snooze, but he'll have to wake up soon. There is more fighting to do.

DEFENDING HIS HOME

Kong has a short stint of slaughter to enjoy, and the enemies do all the hard work (coming to him)! Use Kong's fury to deal the most damage and stay safe from the myriad Small Larve that come from the depths to attack him. In fury mode, swats are enough to kill the Small larve without any effort, and the largest of the beasts only take a few dedicated hits to knock into a position where they can be grappled and quickly killed. This helps to prevent Kong from taking much damage.

Any of the Small Larve that leap onto Kong and tangle themselves into his fur are able to cling and bite without fear of easy reprisal. Take the time to grab and throw them off to save Kong.

There are three of the Small Larve, and they are the real targets of the fight (the little guys are there as a distraction). As soon as the fight with the Small Larve ends, the level is completed and the action returns to Jack.

Free!

Run with Ann and do exactly what every parent worries about: jump off a cliff just because she does. Swim with her toward the makeshift raft close by and start the ride off of Skull Island. Ann explains more of her feelings about everything that has happened. There is nothing to put the two in danger in this level, so enjoy the dialogue and take a breather.

Chased

Follow Ann again and slip past the fighting Venatosauruses out in the open plateau. Take the Spears from that area and slay the dinosaur that wins the fight, and kill the creatures that come afterward. Stay near the shelter, even when Ann tries to head off. She'll quickly come back once the Venatosaurus starts approaching her.

The Spears in the area are just outside the shelter where Ann hides and inside another shelter across the way. That far shelter also has a fire, which is needed to destroy the thicket ahead. Doing this while there are still Venatosauruses fighting in the area is useful because they take damage from the flames.

Kong is searching around not too far away after the thicket is destroyed and Ann prepares to leave, but it doesn't seem like he has spotted anyone yet. Stick with Ann and leave the area soon.

Heading back

Hopefully Jack's throwing arm is up for more work, because it's needed here. Accuracy and speed rule the day, as Jack needs to fight several waves of enemies without the benefit of a projectile weapon. Advance carefully with Ann and note the Spear racks along a central road that the two reach (this must be close to more Skull Islander territory). Many predators and scavengers are here, and all of them are ready to feed.

Kill the Venatosaurus that attacks the first creature along the road. Use the distracted time while the dinosaur is nibbling to get the first Spear into its flank, and don't let the thing rise again. Grab the Spear from its body and skewer it again and again with additional throws. Use the trashed Spear afterward to knock the fire urn off of the wall down the road, and choose a new Spear from the rack nearby.

Two smaller Venatosauruses rush forward, coming after Jack and Ann. They only take one hit a piece, so they are not a substantial threat. Also, ignore the creatures ahead, as they won't be an issue for a few more moments. Instead, it's the tougher Venatosaurus that is more ominous. Let Ann advance along while Jack stays near a Spear rack. This is necessary, because the next Venatosaurus is GOING to go after Jack, even if Ann is in front. Use the Spear rack to allow for throwing without advancing to finish the beast at point blank.

THE FRONT END IS THE BUSINESS END

The technique of hitting a Venatosaurus with a Spear and pulling that same Spear out for another throw is NOT safe from the front side of a Venatosaurus. It's too easy for the Venatosaurus to make a sudden recovery from the first strike and nibble on Jack, putting the entire team in jeopardy. Use this technique when Venatosauruses can be outflanked.

The two creatures are next, and they aren't very powerful. Throw at the first from range, before it comes near, and then wait for the second to charge and make an easy target of itself. Finish the level by defeating a rush from several smaller Venatosauruses (they go after both Ann and Jack). Worry about the ones on Jack first, as Ann is surprisingly hardy by this point, and polishes off the others afterward.

To the village

An area of massive overgrowth needs to be cleared, and Jack is not afraid of some fun manual labor. Use the Bones and Spears around the yard ahead to knock the many fire urns off of their resting places. This destroys the offending briars and opens the way around the right perimeter of the yard. A small crack in the left wall is the eventual

target, where Ann and Jack slip through. Not too far ahead is the great wall of the island, where the villagers first captured Ann and Jack. Follow Ann back into the village and watch to see what happens.

Captured

The Skull Islanders are messing with the wrong people, and they are having genuine trouble realizing that hundreds of their people die every time they do something that makes Kong angry. Well, it has happened again, and Kong is just arriving to begin a new lesson.

Tear into the village and look for the concentrations of archers. All of these must be splattered before Kong can push through the main gateway. Break through a barricade on the left side of the village to climb up to the largest concentration of archers, then leap around the right side of the area and down to the lower tier to squish the others. Beyond that, only a few archers stand near platforms by the main gate itself, and they take no more than a second to dispense with. Push the pillar at the gate aside and break through.

Race along, through the next pocket of scaffolding and archers, and out that gateway as well. An area of lava and fire is between Kong and the beach, where he is taking Ann; jump to the central pillar, grab Ann, and leap from there to a series of vines and lead up and out of the region. Place Ann on the stone centerpiece there and wait for her to burn away the brush above with a thrown Spear. When this is done, climb the vines with Ann in hand, and leave the Skull Islanders behind.

After reaching the summit, Kong has a free race to the sea. Ann will be safe with her kind. The rest doesn't seem as important to Kong. He'll figure that out later. Jack has a brief moment to speak with Carl and Ann after the action dies down, then the Venture is ready to leave for New York.

The streets of new york

Angry? Frustrated? Does the world not always provide the things that would make life so much easier? Kong understands. Kong is angry too. Now, Kong is going to do something about it.

Tap the controls several times to shake Kong back and forth. He'll build some strength and rip the cursed chains right out of their supports. Everything quickly turns to chaos in the city, and another rampage begins. The Skull Islanders are just happy that it isn't them taking the heat this time!

Charge through the streets and swat the trivial threats out of the way. Only entire groups of police or military units are able to do anything to Kong. Pick up cars when these dangerous enemies come into sight and throw the vehicles at Kong's foes to destroy them. The military has a couple trucks with anti-tank guns on them, and these are the top-tier targets. Always use ranged attacks against them, to keep things simple.

Spotlights are easy to destroy with hurled cars as well; don't try to climb up to them. It's far better to watch the cars track in on the hapless fools. They should NOT have taken pot shots at Kong in the first place.

Though there are peripheral streets, the path is still linear and fairly direct toward the Empire State Building. A blockade with a heavy bus is in the way, with two spotlights and machinegunners flanking the area. Destroy the spotlights first, to prevent the gunners from interrupting Kong, then lift the bus.

Trucks with anti-tank guns are flanking the run beyond that barricade. There is no reason to destroy each of these, as it takes extra time and doesn't get Kong anything special (though ripping the things to shreds does have a virtue of its own).

Farther down the street, near the Empire State Building, Ann joins Kong and the military trucks pull in behind him. Use the support beam right next to Kong to climb the building quickly and leave the range of the trucks. Don't stop at the first ledge; continue to climb.

Take Ann to the very top of the Empire State Building, then switch from side to side and swat at the prop fighters that come after the mighty Kong. It's a valiant fight, and there is no doubt that Kong must give his all.

BATTLING AGAINST THE IMPOSSIBLE

An endless series of aircraft attacks beset the brave Kong, and he cannot destroy them all. It is only a matter of time before he takes a grave wounding from their incessant fire. Yet, careful tactics make the most of each second, costing Kong's enemies dearly. Stay on a different side of the building from incoming fighters until the last moment, then swing into position for a swipe. This increases Kong's rate of destruction while protecting him somewhat. It's a moral victory, to be sure.

Become a BradyGames® Online

 MEMBER

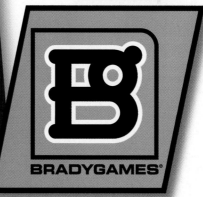

Membership is free, fast & easy!

Register this code on our web site:
0-7440-0548-5

©2006 Pearson Education

BradyGAMES® is a registered trademark of Pearson Education, Inc.

All rights reserved, including the right of reproduction in whole or in part in any form.

BradyGAMES® Publishing

An Imprint of Pearson Education
800 East 96th Street, Third Floor
Indianapolis, Indiana 46240

© 2005 Ubisoft Entertainment. All Rights Reserved. Ubisoft and the Ubisoft logo are trademarks of Ubisoft Entertainment in the U.S. and/or other countries. Universal Studios' King Kong movie © Universal Studios. Licensed by Universal Studios Licensing LLLP. All Rights Reserved. A Note to Parents: Please consult www.filmratings.com for information regarding movie ratings in making viewing choices for children.

The ratings icon is a registered trademark of the Entertainment Software Association. All other trademarks and trade names are properties of their respective owners.

Please be advised that the ESRB ratings icons, "EC", "E", "E10+", "T", "M", "AO", and "RP" are trademarks owned by the Entertainment Software Association, and may only be used with their permission and authority. For information regarding whether a product has been rated by the ESRB, please visit www.esrb.org. **For permission to use the ratings icons, please contact the ESA at esrblicenseinfo@theesa.com.**

ISBN: 0-7440-0548-5

Library of Congress Catalog No.: 2005935310

Printing Code: The rightmost double-digit number is the year of the book's printing; the rightmost single-digit number is the number of the book's printing. For example, 05-1 shows that the first printing of the book occurred in 2005.

09 08 07 06   4 3 2 1

Manufactured in the United States of America.

Limits of Liability and Disclaimer of Warranty: THE AUTHOR AND PUBLISHER MAKE NO WARRANTY OF ANY KIND, EXPRESSED OR IMPLIED, WITH REGARD TO THESE PROGRAMS OR THE DOCUMENTATION CONTAINED IN THIS BOOK. THE AUTHOR AND PUBLISHER SPECIFICALLY DISCLAIM ANY WARRANTIES OF MERCHANTABILITY OR FITNESS FOR A PARTICULAR PURPOSE. THE AUTHOR AND PUBLISHER SHALL NOT BE LIABLE IN ANY EVENT FOR INCIDENTAL OR CONSEQUENTIAL DAMAGES IN CONNECTION WITH, OR ARISING OUT OF, THE FURNISHING, PERFORMANCE, OR USE OF THESE PROGRAMS.

BRADYGAMES STAFF

PUBLISHER David Waybright
EDITOR-IN-CHIEF H. Leigh Davis
DIRECTOR OF MARKETING Steve Escalante
CREATIVE DIRECTOR Robin Lasek
LICENSING MANAGER Mike Degler

CREDITS

DEVELOPMENT EDITOR Chris Hausermann
SCREENSHOT EDITOR Michael Owen
BOOK DESIGNER Carol Stamile